PIECE TO PEACE

A JOURNEY OF HEALING AND SELF-DISCOVERY

CHOLEE ENGLISH

Copyright © 2023 Cholee English

All rights reserved. This publication, or any part thereof, may not be reproduced in any form, or by any means, including electronic, photographic, or mechanical, or by any sound recording system, or by any device for storage and retrieval of information, without the written permission of the copyright owner.

Contents

Chapter 1: How It All Began: A Piece of Confusion 4

Chapter 2: The Broken Piece 12

Chapter 3: A Piece of Rejection: Wounds of Abandonment 24

Chapter 4: A Piece of the Looking Glass: Looking For Love In All the Wrong Places 50

Chapter 5: A Piece of Settling: Marriage, Divorce, and Life After Divorce 65

Chapter 6: A Piece of Redemption: Finding Me 116

Chapter 7: A Piece of Encouragement: The Best Version of Me 125

Chapter 1:

How It All Began: A Piece of Confusion

Born the last child and only girl to my mom, I pretty much had it made. I was spoiled, and I loved it. I was a momma's girl. Of course, being the baby and the only girl meant that momma had fun with me. I was always dressed to the T, with the bonnet hats, white ruffle socks, and shiny shoes, with the purse on my wrist. Being the baby also meant that I had two older, over-protective brothers, who loved me, but sometimes hated how spoiled and how much of a brat I was.

My mom was a single parent, as she had made the decision to leave her husband when she was three months pregnant with me. With her being a single parent, she did what most mothers do; she took on more work. With me being the baby and mom working all the time, I spent a whole lot of time with my grandparents. I remember my grandmother telling me I had been with her since I was three months old. I remember a lot of my early childhood years being spent on Hanover Street. The Honey Comb Hideout is what it was called back then. I would stay at home with mom and my brothers at our home on Wellsley Street at night, then every morning, mom would get ready for work, and she would drive me and drop me off with Granny and Paw Paw. Granny would get me ready for school, and I would either catch the bus or Paw Paw would take me.

During this time, I never really saw my dad around much. It would be once in a blue moon that he would drop in, then he'd disappear again. Later, it became clear that did he spurts in and out of prison. I would get the letters, and they would always have very nice artwork in them. My dad was actually very talented in many areas. He was a singer, a skilled musician that could play any instrument that he put his hands to, and he loved to draw. With mom and dad being divorced for quite some time now, of course, mom had moved on.

Now I really can't remember how this guy came into

play, but I do know that he was there, and he was the most prevalent man in my life. This man was actually the one that I knew and loved as my daddy. I spent so much time with him, his mom, his sisters, and his remaining family. THIS was my family! Because I was so young, I really didn't ask questions, as we were always told to stay in child's place. Like, I knew that mom's ex-husband was my dad and that he was my brother's dad, but this one right here; this particular guy, was mine. He also began to do spurts, but when he was there, he was there. He then began to disappear, and those letters began to trickle in again. Even with my daddy being incarcerated, my grandmother and aunts always made sure that I knew my daddy loved me and that they loved me too. I would always spend the night over at my grandma's or at my aunts' house. They would always make sure that I was available to visit my daddy. I loved the time that I spent with them. Bonds that will NEVER be broken were created.

Have you ever felt reassured about something? Something that no one can sway you of otherwise? Well, that was me. Again, because this was the only man that had ever been there as a dad for me, no one could tell me otherwise. Well, what happens when you get an inkling of something that defies your belief? Yeah, that feeling right there. I remember one day at school when one of my cousins came in with her friends. Of course, I spoke to her, but she didn't respond. As I walked past, I heard her say, "That's not my cousin. We're not really cousins." As a child, yes, we can be really mean and harsh, but that really hurt me because I could not figure out why she would say that. I am her cousin! WE ARE COUSINS! At least, that's what I believed to be true. Had my mom been lying to me? I didn't know what to believe because I was still in elementary school. He was my dad, and she was my cousin, and that was my grandmother, and that was that. But was it really true?

Now things were different when going to Grandma's. Of course, there was that feeling of rejection, and now, insecurity and confusion began to set in. My aunt could tell something was different and asked what was wrong and what had happened. I did tell her about the incident at school. My Aunt exclaimed and said, "YOU ARE COUSINS, and he is your daddy, and nothing will change that!" Then, she gave me the biggest hug ever. That made me feel so good and reassured. Her statement gave me exactly what I needed, and at that very moment. Even though my aunt gave me reassurance, that did not alleviate the confusion that was caused by my cousin's statement; it just added to the hidden and suppressed confusion about Dad and Daddy. This is where it all began — the Piece of Confusion.

I know that there are some of you that can identify with the beginning of this story, dealing or coping with the fact of being raised in a single-parent home. The second part of this story may even be familiar to some, and it may have caused the same feelings of insecurity, rejection, and confusion. What's important for you to know is that God desires us to have clarity and understanding. He stated that in all we get, we should get an understanding, Proverbs 4:7. He would also not have us to be confused, as He is not the author of confusion, 1 Cor 14:33. I also submit to you that God is so loving to His children, that in the absence of fathers, HE is a father to the fatherless. He knows exactly what part of us needs extra attention and when. If you have any of these feelings, I encourage you to give it all to Jesus. Let His love overtake you and burn out those feelings.

God, we thank you that YOU are a God of love and grace. Thank YOU for being the ultimate father to your children, especially for those of us that did not have fathers in the home. God, we thank you that You are not the author of confusion and that you desire clarity and understanding for Your children. God, we desire to have wisdom, as it is the principal thing. We thank You for healing us of our past hurts and feelings of insecurity, rejection, and confusion. In Jesus' Name. Amen.

Scriptures to Consider

Proverbs 4:7 - Wisdom is the principal thing; therefore get wisdom: and with all thy getting, get an understanding.

1 Corinthians 14:33 – For God is not the author of confusion, but of peace, as in all churches of the saints.

Psalms 68:5 – A father of the fatherless and a judge of the widows, is God in His Holy habitation.

What Did You Take Away From This Chapter?

Chapter 2:

The Broken Piece

Every child dreams of having the perfect home with both mom and dad and the perfect family. Well, as stated in chapter one, that really wasn't how things turned out for me. The closest that I had to that dream was my grandparents, who were my second mom and dad. Even with having them, it just wasn't enough. I needed to have mom and dad in my life.

Now, knowing that there could be some possibility that who I thought was dad wasn't, it was back to just mom. I still got to spend time with my other family and was still treated as though dad number two was really my dad. Nothing really kept me away from them or from him. Aside from it just being mom and my grandparents, I did have aunts and uncles who loved me, as well as godparents, who I also got to spend time with. I saw my godmothers a lot, and I can remember having three, but I only remember two godfathers, and I only remember the actual presence of one. The other pretty much did the same thing as dads one and two; they popped in and out. So, that is kind of what I had gotten used to; men popping in and out of my life.

Mom had gotten word from her workplace that the plant she had worked at for many years would be closing. What was she going to do? How was she going to provide for her family? As a result, she made a decision that would change all of our lives. Mom made a decision to join the Army as a reservist. What would that mean for my brothers and I? Where would we stay? Who would raise us while mom was gone? Well, I really don't know why that was a question because, of course, like always, we would stay with Granny and Paw Paw. We had made all of the necessary changes to move in with our grandparents. My brothers were six and four years older than me, so they were pretty much able to take care of themselves. However, I had to have custody switched from my mom to my grandparents. I really didn't understand too much of the legalities, but what I did know was that legally, I was now Granny and Paw Paw's 9th child and that I would not be going home with mom in the evenings anymore. I did learn that with her being a reservist, she would only be gone for one weekend out of each month and for 18 months out of each year for an overseas tour, with the exception of school to rank higher.

This had a significant impact on me. Even though I finally had two parents raising me now, it still wasn't the same as having my mom and my dad under one roof, raising me. My grandparents were older, so they really didn't get out to anything other than church services. I grew up singing, as I come from a musical family. So, of course, the choir would be the natural elective to choose. When we had performances, of course, I wanted mom and dad to be there, just as other students had, or at least have Granny and Paw Paw there, but that didn't happen either, and that's pretty much how things went all through school up until graduation.

We had fun at Granny's house. Our house was like the neighborhood's house. All the kids in the area would come to our house to play around, to come to the clubhouse, and to pretty much just have a good time. My God, the Hash's, the Simpsons, the Aytons' the Dawsons, the Lovelaces, the

Lynchs', D Waller, Kabara and Ernie, the Williams brothers, Junior Word, V Gibson, the Lees' and the Englishs' came a little bit later. We had the swing set in the back yard, the big empty side yard that was perfect for kickball, dodgeball, volleyball, and badminton when the net was set up. We had hopscotch and double-dutch, and we even tied our bikes to Paw Paw's big red Pee Wee Herman bike and were pulled down the big hill. My brother and the other guys in the neighborhood had a dance group, and they thought they were Kid and Play, lol. The guys would always cut across the highway to get to the Apple Market to get candy. Man, those were the good old days.

Because we were raised in a Christian home, the only form of cards that we were allowed to play were UNO. We had fun doing so, but we had to come up with new ways of doing so. We had to make up our fun. We would have beauty pageants, and talent shows that always somehow led to fights and someone being disappointed. We had to take turns being the winner, but we didn't understand that at the moment.

Because we were in Granny and Paw Paw's and we were in a Christian home, we were raised in the fear of the Lord. We had Bible Study and prayer every night at the dinner table at 7 pm, and if you were in Paw Paw's house, you had better find yourself at that table at 7 pm. There were days that I didn't want to be at the table because I thought it was for old people, and it was boring, and I wanted to be playing with my friend or doing something else. There were, however, other times when I wanted to be apart. I wanted to pray, and I wanted to read the word. This is actually where I learned how to pray and where I gained my love for God and a yearning for a relationship with HIM. This was also around the time when I had made the decision to get baptized. I was about 11.

Some time had now passed, and mom had finished her basic training and had returned home. Even though she had returned, we didn't go back through the courts to change things back because she knew she would be in and out with her military duties. By this time, I was able to move back in with my mom and go to school from her house. It made me happy to be home, but there was still something missing there because mom was always at work, and when she wasn't, she was resting from work and for work again. This meant that I pretty much fended for myself as far as food, well, cooking it at least, which meant that oodles and noodles became my favorite thing to eat.

Around this time, my godfather had moved back to Roanoke from Atlanta, and had actually moved around the corner. I began spending a lot more time with him and my godbrothers, as they lived with him now since he had moved back home. One night, my godfather had to minister in Lynchburg, as he plays the organ and pretty much can play any instrument he puts his hands and mind to. My godbrothers were going as well, and this just so happened to be the night that I met his girlfriend. I wasn't too happy about that because I felt like he was really just coming back into my life, and I felt like we needed some time first, but what did I know? I was just a kid. This particular night, we churched, and then after, we chilled. We kind of hung around for a while and just laughed and enjoyed each other's company.

My godfather wanted to talk to me, but he wanted to talk to me in the office. I figured he just wanted to kind of catch up with me and know what was going on with me. He asked me a few questions, and then he kind of paused and said, "How would you like for me to be your daddy?" I kind of looked confused, with a lot of different thoughts running through my mind. I replied, "I would like that. I guess." I mean, what was I supposed to say? He then said, "I'm your daddy. Ricky is not your dad." Again, I was overwhelmed and flooded with so many different thoughts and feelings. How is this possible? Why have I been lied to for 11 years? Why would anyone keep something like this hidden? What did that mean for me and the family that I knew as my family? So, my cousin was actually telling the truth, and everyone else was lying to me. So, my godfather is actually my father? Does that mean that my godbrothers are actually my brothers and also my cousins? While all this flooded my mind, I was happy because I now had more brothers than just the two by mom. I now had four more older brothers. What made it cool at that moment was that my brothers were all so excited as well. They were so happy to have a little sister. Dad had already told them, so they were just as excited as dad was to tell me.

When we got back to Roanoke, dad and mom talked, and he told her what had transpired that night. She wasn't too happy because she wanted to be a part of the decision-making of when and how to tell me, and she felt that it was something that they should have discussed first. She asked me if I had any questions about it, and at the moment I didn't, because I really didn't know what to ask. As time passed, of course, the questions began to surface. What really happened? Why was this hidden? Were there ever plans to tell me the truth? I didn't know how this would affect me in my adult life, or even if it really would, but I would later find out that it would, and it did.

Now that the truth had been put out there, dad and I spent a lot more time together. I did a lot of traveling with him and my brothers. The guys had created a singing group, and of course, dad was playing the organ for them. It was fun while it lasted, but it didn't last too long. Soon, dad had made the decision to move to Norfolk. So, again, he was another dad that was in and out of my life. I was sad, of course, because I felt that he had just come back into my life, shaken my life up a bit, and then was out again. He also took his girlfriend with him, and soon after, they were married. I had a pretty good relationship with her and her family, as we spent a lot of time together when they lived here in Roanoke. My feelings, however, began to change because I felt like she was taking my dad away from me. Before they moved, dad and his girlfriend had a little girl. I was so happy because I always wanted a little sister. I spent as much time with her as I could while they were here, but after the big move, that was really it. Again, it was something that I was used to. You know the in and out. So, I was just back to that again. Back to the brokenness of not really having a mom, and then the brokenness of having three dads, and all of them popping in and out of my life. Ladies and gentlemen, the broken piece.

While single-family homes are something that may be common, that does not change the effect that it may have on a child. The absence of a parent leaves a void in a child's life that the child seeks to fill with other things, be it drugs, alcohol, sex, gambling, and other toxic traits. There are also nontoxic traits that could be used as well to fill the void, such as writing, poetry, singing, art, and things of that nature; just something that pretty much takes your mind off the pain of not having that parent or not having both parents. While some of these things can be beneficial, I know of a man that is the ultimate heart filler and mender of broken hearts, Psalm 147:3. Even though I didn't have my biological dad; he sent me another one that was there, someone that took the role, and helped to raise me into the woman I am today. Even though mom was gone off and on, I was always provided for and was left in good hands. I didn't have to worry about being shuffled from shelter to shelter or from one foster home to another. I may not have known it at that moment, but looking back, I can truly say, "Thank you,

Lord, for keeping me, and for providing, and for always making ways. Thank you for mending the brokenness when I wasn't even aware of how broken I was. Thank you for being a Good, Good Father." When I changed my perspective about the situation, I could see the situation in a different manner, and through it all, I still say, "Thank you, Lord."

God, I thank you now for Your keeping power. I thank you that you are The Keeper and that You heal the brokenhearted. Thank you, God, for taking the wounds of our past and causing them to work for our good. Your word declares that all things work together for the good of those who love the Lord and are called according to Your purpose. Thank you, Lord, for allowing me and others to take the broken pieces of our past and use them to uplift us and make us better for our purpose and for Your glory. Help us, God, to not be broken for no reason but to be broken before you, withholding nothing. In Jesus' Name. Amen.

Scriptures to Consider

Psalms 34:18 - The Lord is near to the brokenhearted, and saves those who are crushed in spirit.

Psalms 147:3 - He heals the brokenhearted and binds up their wounds.

1 Peter 5:7 – Casting all your care upon him; for he careth for you.

What Did You Take Away From This Chapter

Chapter 3:

A Piece of Rejection: Wounds of Abandonment

I have heard it said that when you have your father in your life as a constant, he is supposed to show you the real meaning of love and what it means to be treated as a lady, a queen/princess, and that this love sets a precedent for how you are to be treated and loved in future relationships. Well, of course, I didn't have that. With the in and out and the confusion between the three dads, that's pretty much what I became accustomed to and what I allowed. Now, please, do not get me wrong, I was loved, and I knew that, and yes, I had the presence of my grandfather, and he was the perfect father for me, but he was older and from a different time.

You know, they really didn't believe in us having boyfriends or being in relationships at early ages or before high school, so they really didn't go into much detail about relationships.

Granny and Paw Paw had been married for many, many years, and they taught us what they knew and what they had been taught. They taught us in the way of the Lord and by Biblical principles. They were great examples of a saved, married couple. My granny was a great housewife. She took care of her husband, her kids/grandkids, and her home. I can remember every day my granny having breakfast for Paw Paw, helping him get ready for work, her having dinner ready when he got home from work. I also witnessed her washing and ironing clothes and making sure that things were in order and in place. I very seldom saw my grandparents fight or argue. Sure, they would disagree on things, and they would be discussed and resolved, and things would be okay. I remember seeing them kiss and seeing my Paw Paw rubbing my granny's feet, and sometimes he would pat her on the bottom and say, "Oh, Mrs. Hash," and she would say in her sweet little voice, "Oh, Marvin." I would just grin from ear to ear when I heard and saw them do this. What I remember most is that they both did things to make and keep each other happy.

I loved my Paw Paw very much. I knew that he loved all of his grandkids, but I was his favorite. How could I not be? I spent the most time with them. For the most part, I had lived with them or shared residence with him and Granny for most of my life. Although I was not fully aware of all of the details of the happening of the dad situations, all of the adults were fully aware. I think that kind of made them feel that I needed extra love and extra care. Even though I felt this way, I knew I was tripping because Paw Paw treated us all the same and loved us all the same, and disciplined us as all the same. However, lol, in my mind, I was his favorite. His Coco Bunch, his Bunchie Munchie. My favorite thing in the world to hear him say to me was, "What do you know, Cocy Co?" I would smile so hard. He was the one that drove me to school every morning, and I sometimes would ride with him to the store to pick up somethings for my Granny. Our morning store runs would consist of a bag of Blow Pops for my Granny, some thing for dinner that night, and maybe a Root Bear and Peanuts for me and Paw Paw. We would make it back from the store just in time for me to get on the bus. Granny would give me a few blow pops to take with me. I always had some candy of some sort on me, and I still always do to this day.

I can remember my grandfather being a mister fix-it. He could fix anything and everything, and what he couldn't, he would call his best friend, Mr. Charlie, over to help him with. I loved watching them fix things. They fixed our bikes, our swing set, our wagons, and pretty much anything that we needed to put together or get fixed. I loved having my grandfather in my life, and I miss him more and more each day, but his presence did not fill the void created by my father's absence. Yes, I had lots of uncles and tons of cousins, but none of them were my father. With my mother still in the military and then also still working, I still spent a lot of time away from home. I had close relationships with my uncles. I was a very good baby-sitter, so a lot of the time, that's what I did. When I babysat, I stayed there.

I don't really remember the full details of one particular night, but what I do remember is being in bed wearing a long t-shirt and underwear. One of my uncles was in bed with me, and he placed his arm around me as if to hold me. His hand began to move down my stomach towards my private area. He didn't go all the way to my private area, but he stopped at my pelvic region and just began to rub. I felt weird, but as a kid and as one that was taught to obey her elders, what was I really to say or do? I'm grateful that it didn't go any further than it did, but it still had an impact on me that still affects me to this day. When what had happened became known, I was blamed for it. The statement that was made to me was, "I told you about sleeping with grown men." I think that statement broke me and hurt me most of all. How could I be blamed for this? I caused this to happen to myself? I wasn't the adult in the situation.

I don't think that I looked at this person the same anymore, which really hurt me because this person meant so much to me. It really hurt me to be looked at like I was some fast tail girl that got what she deserved. So, because I was looked at that way, that's how I began to look at myself. No, I didn't start sleeping around, but I had the thoughts in my mind. I had a lot of boyfriends, but not all at the same time. When I was in a relationship, I was in a relationship, meaning that mostly all of the relationships I had were long-term. In my 40 years of living, I have had eight serious relationships, and seven of them were long-term, meaning six months plus. Out of the eight, there have been about three that meant the most and that have had the most lasting impact. I guess you could say that I was looking for love in these relationships. You know, the love I was missing from not having a steady father/daughter relationship. It's been said that when I love, I love hard, and this statement is very true. So, when I called myself falling in love, I fell hard and allowed just about anything from the one that I fell for.

I was in one particular relationship for about 12 years, off and on. We first started dating when we were kids, and we really didn't know too much about it but were just able to say that we were boyfriend and girlfriend. We had already known each other, as our families had grown up together. He felt it would be easy for him to talk to me as his first cousin was my half-brother. Yes, his first cousin was one of the brothers I didn't know I had. We dated for a little bit, and then we broke up. He said I dumped him for another guy and broke his heart. I think that it's a possibility, but highly unlikely. Some years passed, and we somehow ended up back together, lol. By this time, we were a little older and knew a little more about what we wanted. I was a Junior in High School and was on the Homecoming Court. He saw me, and of course, I was flawless and gorgeous! This time, he approached his mom and my brother about me. I told them that he needed to come to me himself, and he did, and we began dating again. I did, of course, think that it was just him and I, and I felt that way for such a long time. We spent so much time together. I would meet him at his grandparent's house, or I would go to his house and hang out. Of course, my family loved him, and his family loved me, and they loved the thought of us being together. My Granny was the happiest. She absolutely loved this guy. She just knew in her head that we were going to be together forever. Thinking back on it, I did too.

Little did I know, I wasn't his only girlfriend. I had actually found out that he had a girlfriend in every zip code and probably had more physical partners than that. At some point, I found out about all of them, whether it was from him or from other sources. It did hurt to find out that he had been lying to me for so long and about multiple people, but I was so gone over him that I didn't want to let him go. I found out that he had been dating one for about the same amount of time that he had been dating me, and then I found out that he had been dating another girl for the same amount of time that he had been dating us. I couldn't believe it. We all had beef and tension between us for a long time, and then the first girl and I resolved it and let it go. We actually became close after that. Anyhow, we continued dating, and during this time, I fell deeper and deeper in love with him. Around this time, I had just turned 18 and was about to graduate high school. For my birthday, I decided to lose my virginity to him, and I did. After that point, I was completely gone. It didn't matter what he did to me and how much it hurt me; I did not want to let him go. I mean, he brought more girls around me, even got two of them pregnant, oh, but if I mentioned another guy, or if he found out about another guy, it would be a big deal. At one point, he told me to go ahead and date other people because he was going to continue to date other girls, but at the time, I didn't want to date anyone else; I wanted him. I loved him. I was in love with him. Even though he said that, he didn't mean it. We were always arguing about the stuff that he was doing, but it didn't matter to him.

It wasn't until I was about 23 years old that I finally decided to let it and him go and move on. I had been hurt and damaged so much that I was tired. It had gotten to the point that it was making me unstable. The bad thing was that I could not get away from him because we had to see each other at practices and at church. It had gotten so bad that I was pulling out of the parking lot of practice one night, and he was right there in the path, and I sped up and tried to run him over. I can't say that I don't know what came over me because I do. The hurt, the pain, all the girls, the pregnancies. Oh, my goodness. It took me so long to fully and completely let him go and really be healed and move on with my life. I had to pray hard for this soul tie to be broken from my life. I had promised myself that I would never allow myself to be treated like that ever again by anyone.

The next relationship was for about three years. I have to say that this was probably the best relationship that I had, but I was the problem. The problem was I didn't know how to be in a functional relationship. I had a very bad attitude and was stubborn. We loved to wrestle, but sometimes I would take things too far. My smart mouth would always get me in trouble, and he would let me know. He was different from what I had before, and I definitely mistreated him. I was abusive to him verbally and physically. Besides that, our relationship was good. My mom had met him, and she liked him based on the few times that she had seen him, and I had met his mom and stepdad, and we had a good relationship. He was an artist, and he would always draw pictures of me and do little things for me to make me smile. Because of what I had gone through in the twelve-year relationship, I didn't trust him. If I felt like he possibly was messing with someone else, I took things overboard. I made things more than what they really were, even when there was nothing. This one really did love me, and yes, the feeling was mutual. When I saw him talking to another female, I blew that entire situation out of proportion. I began to bully and taunt the female that I thought he was cheating with. In reality, he was not messing with her, but because of my behavior and my mouth, I pushed him into a relationship with someone else. I couldn't believe it. It hurt me so badly because I didn't really think he would leave me, and I didn't think he would actually leave for good and not come back.

Looking and thinking back, I can honestly say that I lost a good one to my stubborn behavior and to my bad attitude. That was definitely a lesson learned. This relationship forced me to look at myself and ask some hard questions. Why was I so abusive? What made me treat him the way that I did? I later found out that my mom was a victim of domestic violence, and that's why she left her husband when she was pregnant with me. I guess it somehow had some reverse effect on me as to why I didn't want to be a victim, so I would abuse them before they had the chance to abuse me. The only thing is that I didn't do it in every relationship. Now, my strong attitude and stubbornness follow me, but the physical part of it was something that only happened in this relationship. It amazes me how something I didn't remember or even see could affect me. This guy and I attempted to rekindle after many years, and it probably would have worked, but I made a choice not to. We still see each other and are cordial with one another.

The last relationship of the three was the longest of them all. We started out as friends, as our families had also grown up together, and our churches fellowshipped together. Being that I was raised pretty much by my grandparents and always at their house, he and his family had moved around the corner. After finding out about my half-brothers, I had a really close relationship with two of them around my senior year of high school and after. We were very close and did a lot of things together. We were pretty much inseparable. My brother had put together a group that the three of us were a part of, and this guy was a musician in the group. Of course, he was close to my brothers, so that gave him access to me. I had never looked at him as anything more than a friend, owing to the fact that he was married, and I respected that. When I was approached about him, I immediately said, "NO!" Even though I was adamant about my NO, I was still approached about him multiple times.

I began to see the situation differently, not as him wanting to hook up with me, but as me being a friend to him.

I became pretty much a sounding board and a really close friend. My intentions were pure. There was no hidden agenda for me. We would talk every day. We would email, text, and call. We started our morning off with prayer emails, and eventually, his aunt joined in. It had actually come to the point where he began to discuss the issues that he was having in his marriage. I couldn't identify as a wife, but I could identify as a woman. I began to offer different ways of looking at the situations that were being described to me and also attempted to offer different actions to take other than those that had already been taken. All of the methods that I had offered had already been tried. From that point, all I could really do was continue to be his sounding board and pray. Although his intentions may not have been the purest with his initial reason for wanting to talk to me, he had gotten to know me. As I said, we had known each other before, but not on a personal level. We spent a lot of time together, but never alone. We were always about 3-6 people deep. We would get together and sing; the guys would jump on the instruments and play, depending on where we were praying, and just have a good time together. It had gotten to the point that we would go to "The Clouds" at 5 am for prayer. It was what we needed at the time because all of us were going through something.

The more time we spent with one another, the more we got to know one another. And the more we got to know one another, the more we began to fall in love with who the other person was. While at the time, he and his wife were having issues and had separated for a bit, they had decided to reunite and work through the issues. This was the goal and what we had been working towards, so as his friend, I stepped back and allowed him to do what he needed to for his family. We had no contact for about two years, it seemed. Surprisingly, we didn't even see each other during this time, which was fine because I continued living my life as well. One night after church, a dear friend and I were riding around town, and we were at a stop sign about to cross the street, but we were stopped by an oncoming car. To our surprise, it was he and his cousin who used to hang out with us. They had just gotten out of church as well and were about to go get some food when they asked where we were headed and if we had any plans, and we pretty much told them we didn't and were also looking for something to eat. We decided to meet up somewhere to eat and catch up. My friend and I went our way to get food, and they went their way to get food, and we met up at a central location. We gave each other the biggest hug when we were finally able to stop and get out of the car, as it had been about two years since we had seen or heard from each other. The four of us stayed in the parking lot for a while, talking, laughing, and catching up. We had no idea we were being followed and someone had been watching us. I am unsure if they stayed for the entire interaction, but I know that they followed us to where we met. Because they did see us meet up, it was reported to his wife. Of course, the entire situation was blown completely out of proportion, as they all were, and I soon would discover just how much.

During this time, so much was going on at my church that we were losing members left and right. It had come to the point where I had made a decision to leave my home church. This was a very vulnerable time because things were being revealed about my Spiritual father that I could not and did not want to believe. The honest thing is that I would not have believed it had I not been approached by him myself. And the thing about it was that I was so blinded by him being my spiritual father and like an actual father to me that I did not take the things he was saying to me as inappropriate. It was not until I received a call from my brother and former armor bearer to the Pastor, stating that he and his wife had left the ministry and were warning me and advising me to be careful if I continued to go. This actually ripped my heart into pieces in so many different ways because the church that I was born and raised in was literally being torn apart piece by piece, and I had to leave somewhere I thought I would always be. Second, the man I had trusted my life with, my spiritual life and growth, had not only betrayed me and my trust but also so many others. He was supposed to be a man of dignity, integrity, and a leader. I mean, this man was literally a walking, living, breathing Bible. How? Why?

At this point, I knew I was never going back there, but I knew that I wasn't going to stop going to church. It was at this time that I had a really big decision to make. I needed to find a church to visit so that I could begin searching for a new church home. At this time, my spiritual walk was good. I was rooted, I was planted, and I was in the word every day, and I was praying every day. I was a worship leader at the church, but now I was having to start all over. I remember pretty much crying myself to sleep over the last four days, praying, and asking God to lead me where he wanted me to be. I also knew that I didn't want to follow my brother and his wife because I no longer wanted to be under his shadow, but I wanted to be known as Cholee, not just Vernon Jr's or Rico's little sister, as I was so often referred to. I remembered that about a week or so prior, when I ran into my friend, he gave me his updated phone number. I called him to find out where their church was located and what the service times were, but I didn't receive an answer. I had decided on one of two churches. If my friend contacted me back, then it would be there, and if not, then I would go where my brother and sister-in-law were, and that was with our spiritual advisor. Later that evening, my friend called me back and gave me the information I had requested, and that's where I went the next day. Service was really good, and it really met me where I was. The word and the teaching were on the level that I needed them to be, especially coming from where I had come from. I did not join that day. After praying and visiting for a few more weeks and after making sure that it was a good fit for me, I then joined. I wanted to just sit and be ministered to first before actually being put to work, but, yeah, it didn't work like that. I was immediately recruited to the Praise and Worship team.

Being that I was recruited to the Worship team, that meant that I would have to communicate and interact with my friend, as he was the minister of music. This means that in his wife's mind, I was a threat. I made sure that I stayed in my place and only talked to him when it had to do with the P&W team, but she didn't see it like that. Anytime she saw us talking, she automatically thought it was about a relationship or us being disrespectful to her, which led to me being summoned into the Pastor's office. It also was the first time I fought in church. Yes, I was and am saved, but I'm not stupid, and I'm not a punk, either. I remember having to discuss services and whether or not I would be there when we were at a conference and music was being discussed. Of course, because we were talking, assumptions were being made. After speaking with him regarding the music, I began walking out while speaking with another gentleman that was walking out with me. By the time I got to my car, I was approached by this woman who yelled at me and called me out, and we had a fight in the parking lot. She ran up to me, and I pushed her off of me and out of my face and explained that nothing was going on and that I was not scared of her. By this time, he had been made aware of what was going on, and others had heard the commotion outside and had come running. When he came out and saw us fighting, he came running, grabbed her, and they began to fight. Of course, she was upset because it appeared as though he was defending me. I can only say that this incident was not the first, and it most certainly was not the last. I have had my share of being called into the Pastor's office to please her and to make her happy. And believe that every time was being counted and marked against her. The more confrontation we had, the more his heart and mind turned away from her.

Now, even though our conversation in public remained about business, that didn't mean that we didn't have private conversations. After everything that had happened and all of the previous years of acting out before I even entered the picture, he realized he was tired and no longer wanted to be in that relationship. He had decided that he was in love with me and that he wanted to be with me. We did not officially start dating until he was divorced, and according to her, when he divorced her, he divorced his kids too, but that was so far from the truth. During that time, we got to know so much more about each other, our families, our likes, dislikes, and our dreams and goals. We had real dates, but I also respected the fact that he was a father to his sons, and I gave him the time that he needed with them. When it was us, it was us, and when it was his time with them, it was just that. Of course, there was interference from her, and also some from his family who didn't really know the truth of what had happened or how we started, but all they knew was what they saw or what she had told them. So, of course, I was looked at like a homewrecker, a whore, the one who stole her husband. Yes, it hurts me to be looked at this way, especially by church people, the ones who are not supposed to judge, but they are the ones who turn out to be the most judgmental. I mean, I would get the looks, the eye rolls, and even had people come to me and tell me that I was wrong, and again, they didn't have a clue of anything that had gone on, just what they had heard, or what she had told them. I had been in and out of the Pastor's office so much dealing with her being petty that I decided to leave the church. It had gotten so bad to the point my mom said that if I was called into the office one more time, she was coming up there. Now, anyone who knows my mom knows that she is quiet and reserved and that it takes a whole lot for her to get upset, but do not mess with her children. I'm like my mom in some ways, but not all. I take a lot, and in this situation, I took a lot for his sake and his peace. I understood that how he felt would, in turn, affect our relationship as well, and so did she.

I remember one Wednesday night, we were in Bible Study, and before this Sarcoid really began to surface, I carried around a bag that had my belongings in it, you know, my wallet, keys, Bible, notebook, etc. We were split into rooms in the church per age group. At this particular time, she was not a member, as she had decided to leave the church, but the Sunday before, she decided to join back as a watch care member. The Red Flags in my head started going off because I knew she was up to something. I already saw it coming. I was walking into one of the classrooms, and she was coming out, so I grabbed my bag and put it in front of me so it wouldn't hit her. Well, she purposely bumped into me, so the bag fell from my shoulder and hit her. I said excuse me, grabbed my bag, and kept going. After church, I got called into the Pastor's office. She had gone and told the Pastor that I intentionally hit her with my bag. I couldn't do anything but laugh because, as previously stated, I knew it was coming. So, it was me, him, her, their two sons, the Pastor and Elect Lady, and one of the Elders. Of course, they let her speak first. She says, "I don't know who you think you are, but I'm not scared of you, and I will not be disrespected." Tears were welling up in my eyes because I was furious. She then begins to go into the spill of him choosing to leave her for me and him divorcing "them" and not "her." She says all that she has to say, and then they give me the floor. My response is, "I don't care who you are. I'm not scared nor intimidated by you." I began to tell them what really happened in the room instead of the made-up version that she told them and also the version that she told the oldest son to tell them. I also told them that it was his choice to leave her, and if he wanted to go back, then he was more than welcome to do so. I advised everyone in the office that if that was his decision, I would support it, and I would still love him because that's what a true friend does. It was at that moment when his parents/Pastor and Elect Lady realized that I really did love him and just how much I did. It was also at that point that they realized that I am not a pushover or some timid little girl who is going to roll over and just take anything.

He was then given a chance to speak, and it was then that he made it clear to everyone in the room that he was happy where he was and that he was not going back to her. He stated that he loved his children and would continue to father them, but that he loved me and was going to move forward with me. We were asked if there was anything else that needed to be said, and I chose to say something else. I had the oldest son look at me, and I said, "Your father did not leave you for me. That is a lie, and I don't care who told you that. Your father loves you, and so do I. I love you because of how much your father loves you. Don't believe anything other than what we're telling you right now. Your father loves you and will always be there for you and your brother. Do you hear me?" His response was, "Yes". She didn't like it, but she didn't say anything. The meeting was over, and everyone but her apologized for the senseless meeting. Of course, the foolishness did not end, and there were many more battles that had to be fought. All of this should have been Red Flags and warnings of what was to come and for me to run, but I didn't. I stayed, and I chose to be there with him through this change for five years until we decided to spend the rest of our lives together. My love for him and the time we spent together already outweighed the bad times and all the drama that I had already endured. Could it be? Could it be that accepting all of this drama is a wound of abandonment? Could it be that accepting and allowing all the bad and abusive treatment are all wounds of abandonment? If I had **MY** dad in my life to really love me and show me how I should be treated as a lady and loved by a man, would I have accepted all that I did? If I had the steady presence of my mom and of the men who agreed to love me as their own daughter in my life at an early age and throughout, would things have been different?

I know that for me, I experienced a lot of in and out and back and forth and received wounds from those that were supposed to love me, nurture me, and lead me. I also know that this left me feeling betrayed and unworthy of being loved. It left me with a lot of questions. Why were these things happening to me? What did I do to make these things happen to me? How could I be so stupid to let some of these things happen to me and continue living in the cycle of it all? What I hope that you take away from this is, as I too have taken away, is that God knows our ending from the beginning. He knows the thoughts that he thinks towards us, plans of a hope, and a future. Jeremiah 29:11. Even when we can't see our way through the trees, he already knows what lies ahead. Even though I would never have thought of or seen any of these things happening in my life, HE did. He has promised us that He will never leave nor forsake us, Deuteronomy 31:8. He's also promised that He would heal and bind up our wounds, Psalms 147:3. It doesn't matter what caused the wounds or how long they have been there, God is a restorer of His people. If you're out there, and you're in pain, please allow the power and the love of the Holy Ghost to come in and fill the voids and heal and remove the pain. It is not something that can be done in our own might but something that only God can do.

    God, we are grateful that you chose to love and save a wretch like us. We are so unworthy of your righteousness, but you see fit daily to give it to us anyway. We thank you that your mercies are new every morning. We thank you that even in our mess, and even when we don't make the best decisions for our lives, you are still there to pick up the pieces with loving arms to nurture and heal us back to life. We thank you, Lord, that you are a gracious God who binds up the wounds of unforgiveness, hatred, rejection, abandonment, and abuse. Lord, open our eyes so that we may see ourselves as you see us, God. God, we thank you that you are restoring every reader even now in their hearts and in their minds. Give them the peace, and sweet assurance God, that you have it all in control. God, help us to first forgive ourselves so that we can, in turn, forgive those that have hurt us deeply. Break the chains of bondage caused by unforgiveness and begin to pluck out any residue left. Fill those places with your love, your joy, your peace, and most of all, your word. We thank you in advance for the newness of life that is being birthed in every reader right now, in Jesus' Name. Amen.

Scriptures to Consider

Jeremiah 29:11 – For I know the thoughts that I think toward you says the Lord, thoughts of peace and not of evil, to give you future, and a hope.

Psalms 147:3 – He healtheth the broken in heart, and bindeth up their wounds.

Pslams18:8 – The words of a talebearer are as wounds, and they go down into the innermost parts of the belly.

Jeremiah 30:17 – For I will restore health unto thee, and I will heal thee of thy wounds, saith the Lord; because they called thee an outcast, saying," This is Zion," whom no man seeketh after.

Deuteronomy 31:8 – And the Lord, He is the one who goes before you; He will be with you, He will not leave you nor forsake you; do not fear nor be dismayed.

What Did You Take Away From This Chapter

_____

_____

_____

_____

_____

_____

_____

_____

_____

_____

_____

_____

Chapter 4:

A Piece of the Looking Glass: Looking For Love In All the Wrong Places

~~~~

Aside from the few relationships mentioned in the previous chapter, I have had other relationships. I must say that I've had my fair share. I guess you can say that I was looking for someone to love me, and in a majority of the relationships, most of the guys did. When I went into the relationships, I went in with the intention of longevity. Of course, every young woman dreams of getting married, having kids, and having the perfect home and family. So, yes, that was what I envisioned in my head. I had it all planned out. I was going to be married by the time I was 25, have a good job, and have twins, preferably a girl and a boy, to knock it all out at once. I have heard it said that if you want to make God laugh, tell him your plans. Clearly, HE was laughing at me.

Although my plans haven't happened the way I wanted them to, I still have those dreams, minus being married at 25 and with a few adjustments here and there. Yes, I still long to be married and to have a companion that walks beside me and that is thrilled by the very essence of me. One that honors me and leads me as the head of the family should. The problem was that I was looking for a good man to love me, but I really didn't know what that looked like. All I knew was that if we were committed to each other and showed love and affection to one another, we were good. It wasn't until I started getting older that I realized that there was more. Of the guys that I dated, there were some that were from the church and then some that were not. Of course, I wanted to date the ones that were in the church because we had more in common. I had been brought up in the church, so that's what made sense to me. When dating guys outside of the church, I couldn't get them to understand how it was a major part of my life, and if they were going to be a part of mine, then they would have to accept it. Some had a problem with it, and a couple did not.

As you can imagine, those were the ones that always turned out to be long-term relationships, so it would always be hard when we broke up and decided to go our separate ways. Why? You may ask. It would be hard because when I love, I love hard, and I give my all. What does that mean? It means that I would have a really tough time letting go of the relationship, and I would always end up with my feelings hurt and heartbroken.

I didn't know how to deal with the pain or the hurt that I was feeling. Some things that really hurt me deeply, I keep deep inside and try to bury them so that I don't have to think about them or deal with them. I had so many issues suppressed on the inside that I had to find some way to deal with it all. I remember my mom being deployed to Germany as if she hadn't already been gone before, and she missed a lot of things that I wanted her to be there for. Like before, she left me with my grandparents. Being older and legal now, I didn't want to do that because I knew the rules, and I was now old enough to do things that I wanted to, but I knew wouldn't be allowed to in my grandparents' house. The first thing was that no one my age was there anymore. So I was bored. I probably stayed for a couple of weeks before my aunt invited me to stay with her and her kids.

That was okay with my grandmother. Well, in the course of my staying with my aunt, she allowed me to go hang out at one of my older cousin's houses, and I pretty much called that home. I stayed there all the time. I went back to my aunt's to pretty much check in and say that I was still in her care, but I wasn't. She knew where I was and trusted who I was with. I have to say, that was one of the best times of my life. I gained relationships with people that I will always have and kinships that I'm so grateful for because they came at a very important time in my life.

This was an experimental time and phase for me, and this is when I began to do things to cope. Back then, I didn't know what I was trying to do or what I was actually doing, but this was when I started smoking marijuana and attempted drinking. I will admit that alcohol is not my forte. I began to learn what I could and could not take and what I did and did not like. But baybee, Mary Jane was good to me. I had NEVER SMOKED it before, nor cigarettes, but yes, I did try Newports and quickly found that they were not for me, and I have never smoked a cigarette since. But as far as MJ, she was my friend. When I first hit her, I choked, but the more I hit her, the more comfortable I got. I never got to the point where I was blowing it out my nose and all that, and I never wanted to, but I definitely go lit up. It became something that I did every day. My girl TL and I would get up, get dressed, clean up, and gather our funds so that we could walk to the store and get out two beef hot dogs for $1.00, my bag of cool ranch Doritos, and her Nacho Cheese, my Dr. Pepper, and her Pepsi. In total, it all came to $3.00. Man, those were the good days. We would later chill out with the kids, and the neighborhood crew, as the majority of everyone came to Lucerne to hang out. Big cousin would later fix dinner, or TL would, and we would have such a good time just geeking and laughing with one another. It definitely took my mind off everything that I had buried on the inside, and trust me; I wasn't really thinking of it at all. That was until nighttime rolled around, and the slow jams started going. Back then, Mary J. Blige's Share My World album was in heavy rotation and had your girl all in her feelings. I would lie on the couch high a kite, crying, wishing he would return to me. The sad thing is, I knew he wasn't because I had done him so wrong. Me and my mouth, of course, and when I get ticked off, I talk and fly off the handle. I've gotten better, but it's a process. LOL. But the pain was still there no matter how much I talked, smoked, or drank. I still had the confusion. I still had the void, and I still yearned to be loved. None of it made momma come home; none of it made Dad 1, 2, or 3 love me any more or show up more or less than they had in the past. It didn't bring any of the past guys back.

At some point, thoughts of suicide crept in. I felt like I didn't want to be here anymore. I would sometimes come from the neighbor's next to my cousin's house really late because I would just want to be alone. I would listen to music and just write. I would think, "I wish someone would just come to kill me now while I'm walking from Ole Girl's house." There would be times that I would walk to the park and stay there alone, late, and wish someone would come and just kill me. Times I would think about jumping from the apartment buildings or just simply taking pills. Of course, none of those things happened; glory be to God. Of course, during all of this, I fell all the way off with my spiritual walk. I had been churched so much that I didn't want to hear anything about church. If my Granny asked, I would just tell her that I was going to church with my cousin.

At this time, I did have a relationship with my father, but not really. I didn't talk to him on a regular, but every once in a while. He and his wife were on baby #2, and I had another little sister. Mom had come home from Germany, but she didn't come back alone, and I didn't like it. She had been courted while she was away, and she pretty much was in love, and I hated it because I didn't know him and knew nothing about him. Even with my mom being away, I was still spoiled and was still considered to be Momma's Baby, and I believed this new person was cutting in on my time and my territory. Now, I felt that she was wrong about this. She's already been in and out, and now I had to share her with another person, not to mention my two brothers and the rest of the family. I really was not taking this too well. I tried to either stay occupied or stay away as much as possible. Now, I really started smoking weed. I had my circle of friends from school, and we would have about 5-6 going at one time, being passed around the room. It made some people hungry, it made some people goofy, and others slow, but it made me goofy and sleepy. It would completely mellow me out. As I said before, it didn't make any of my problems disappear, but it made me forget about them in those moments.

Mom continued dating this man, and eventually, during one of the roughest times in our lives, he proposed to her, and she said yes. On the one hand, I was glad that my mom had someone to love and someone to love her back, as she's an amazing woman, but on the other hand, there were still reservations. My mom was very independent and could take care of herself, so what exactly was this man bringing that she couldn't do for herself? After some time, I eventually warmed up to him, as long as my mom was happy. There were a lot of good times that were shared and a lot of good advice that he offered as a father, being that he had become a father figure. Things were not always good, as we did have some times when we were both just downright petty to one another. There were times that he attempted to enforce rules on me that were not needed as I was of age and beyond the point of having some of those rules. You know, rules such as a curfew. Really?!? I was 18 at the time. My mom and I had established that as long as she knew where I was and as long as I wasn't coming in at ungodly hours, then I was fine. Well, he attempted to impose rules beyond that, and it just didn't sit well with me. It was clear that I wasn't going to get the love that I needed from him as a father figure because he was bringing a militant attitude into our situation, and when I say militant, I mean controlling and overbearing. Mom didn't agree with everything that he was attempting to do, but with him being her husband and the head of the household, she went along with it. I understood it to some degree, though.

They were married for a few years before divorcing because the militant, controlling, and other behaviors surfaced and began to take over. A part of me was happy because I had my mom back, but then another part was sad, as well as upset because my mom had been hurt. Yes, I am the child, but that is a hurt that I never want to see. I never want to see my mom hurt, in any way, by anyone.

About 11 years had passed, and mom was away at school. She had now become full-time military, and school was required to rank up. After those, she was stationed away in another city to fulfill the role of her job duties. During this time, she reunited with her ex-husband, and they ended up spending more time together, getting to know one another again. Mom realized that she loved him and that there was no one else out there for her that had the same likes and dislikes as she did. She felt that with time, they both were able to grow and learn from past mistakes. In the beginning, I was completely against it. I didn't like it and didn't like the thought of it. I didn't want my mom to put her heart back into this and be hurt again. Mom sat all of us down, and we had a family discussion about it. She told us how she felt and shared her heart. I was still against it, but if it's what my mom wanted and if it was going to make her happy, then okay. I knew that she was going to do what she wanted to do either way, but the fact that she came to us and we discussed it as a family meant everything. They ended up remarrying, and things were good. We were a family again. We had good times, and mom was happy. We laughed, shared, had family time and family dinners, and just enjoyed being together. It was great until it wasn't.

As you probably have guessed, I was back at home, at the family house. Oh, and yes, I had stopped smoking altogether. It wasn't difficult. I had made up my mind that I wanted to stop, so I did. I was also back in church, and my relationship was stronger than it had been in the time that I was disconnected. I still maintained my close relationship with my cousins and was still there all the time; I just didn't sleep there as much. Even with having all these ins and outs and pop-up dads and whatnot, I later realized that even though I felt that I was void of it, I was surrounded by love the entire time. I didn't and hadn't yet realized that what I had been looking for, I had all along. First, I had the Greatest love of all, the Greatest love of a father, the love of God. Second, I had the love of not one, not two, but three families. I don't know why God chose to give all of them to me or why He felt that I needed them all, but HE knew, and I'm so grateful for each and every person that makes up my family, whether they be Hash, Reynolds, Manns, or Williams. I haven't always had that testimony, but that's for another time.

I know, I know. Some of you may be saying, "You can't find permanency in temporal things." I know that now, but I didn't at the time. As I previously stated, I was looking for something that was going to mask the pain or make me forget about it for a while. I couldn't see the situations changing while I was in them. The Bible tells us not to look to things that are seen, for they are temporal and subject to change, 2 Corinthians 4:18. It also tells us to forget those things that are behind and press forward toward the mark of the high calling of Jesus Christ, Philippians 3:13-14. I know that we all deal with things of our past that try to continuously haunt us and our future, but we have to encourage ourselves and speak life to ourselves. We have to cast down imaginations, wickedness in high places, principalities, and powers, and all that exalts itself against the knowledge of God, Ephesians 6:12.

The best way that I can put it is that we have to see things in a different manner. We have to look at the glass and choose to see it as half full instead of half empty, and yes, at times, this can be hard to do, but we have to make a decision that we want better for ourselves and choose to go after that better. We are able to shape our lives into what we want them to be by speaking things into existence. If we want love, call love into being. If we want peace and happiness, then we should call these things into existence. Not only do we have to speak, but we have to put action behind those words, for the Bible tells us that faith without works is dead, James 2:14, 17. What does that mean? That means that when calling love into existence, we have to do the work on ourselves that could be blocking love from finding us. Humble ourselves, evaluate ourselves, and see where there's room for us to change and grow. Only when we do these things will we begin to see changes begin to manifest in our lives, and we will be able to look back at all that we've come through and laugh and give thanks for God allowing us to make it through.

God, we thank you for seeing us beyond where we see ourselves. We are grateful for your righteousness that sees us the way you created us because we know that our righteousness is as filthy rags. Thank you, Lord, for loving us in spite of ourselves. We thank you, Lord, that you are the Greatest gift of love that was given to us. Open the eyes of our understanding to see that your love is always there. Help us to return to our first love and to understand that once we do so, once we become so consumed with your love, you will begin to fill us with all that we need. Your word tells us that you have given us everything that we need that pertaineth to life and godliness. Help us to see that You know what's best for us, even when we don't see our way. God, You are the way, the truth, and the life. God, heal our hearts so that we are not continuously looking for things that you have already freely given to us. God, we continuously give you thanks and praise for not seeing us as who we were but who you have called us to be. For not allowing our past mistakes to define who we are and what we will become. We thank you that we can use the things of our past for lessons in the future. We can't thank you enough for not turning us over to a reprobate mind and for not taking your hand of mercy from us. We thank you because you are a God of grace, you're faithful, and you're always providing for us. God, we thank you for ordering our steps, for your word says that the steps of a good man are ordered by the Lord. God, we trust you, and we thank you for being a good, good father. It's in Your name that we pray, Amen.

Scriptures to Consider

2 Corinthians 4:18 – So we fix our eyes not on what is seen, but on what is unseen, since what is seen is temporary, but what is unseen is eternal.

Philippians 3:13-14 - Brothers and sisters, I do not consider myself yet to have taken hold of it. But one thing I do: Forgetting what is behind and straining toward what is ahead, I press on toward the goal to win the prize for which God has called me heaven ward in Christ Jesus.

Ephesians 6:12 – For our struggle is not against flesh and blood, but against the rulers, against the authorities, against the powers of this dark world and against the spiritual forces of evil in the heavenly realm.

James 2:14, 17 – What good is it, my brothers and sisters, if someone claims to have faith but has no deeds? Can such faith save them? In the same way, faith by itself, if it is not accompanied by action, is dead.

What Did You Take Away From This Chapter

Chapter 5:

A Piece of Settling: Marriage, Divorce, and Life After Divorce

After dating for five years and being friends even longer, we both decided that we wanted to spend the rest of our lives together. We were sure that this was what we wanted to do, so we went to his parents to let them know of the decision we had made and also for counseling. The number one thing that was made clear to us was that it was not going to be easy, but we could make it as long as we vowed to keep God first and as long as we vowed to love and trust one another. We both knew it would not be easy because of what we had already gone through with just dating. One thing that we had promised to do was not hang onto anything longer than 20 minutes. We made this vow because we were both stubborn, but we didn't want to waste time being mad at each other. The point was to not hold grudges against one another. It worked in the beginning, but not for long.

After counseling, we chose a date, and the planning began. I tried to involve him in every aspect of the planning, but, of course, I received some pushback. I tried to include just about everyone that was close to him in the wedding, but things didn't work that way either. He had people that he didn't want in, and then he had reservations about it all from the start, but he didn't share those with me. Because of the resistance that I was getting, I should have seen what was really going on, but I didn't, but others could. Those that could didn't say anything to me because they didn't want me to feel as though they were trying to ruin my day. We chose the day that we did so that it would be a weekend that he would have his sons around, so they could be a part of the wedding, but somewhere down the road, he decided he didn't want them in it. I had to find a minister for the ceremony because he didn't want his dad to do it, which was another sign, so we just had him do the prayer, and my God-Mother and Pastor of one of the local churches performed the ceremony. His sister and nieces didn't want to be a part of the wedding for their own reasons, which hurt me, but it wasn't about them. It was our day, and nothing was going to stop that.

It then came down to the point where I was scheduling the appointment for the guys to get fitted for their tuxedos and having to call to see when they would go to get fitted, and I wasn't receiving responses from them. At the last minute, guys were being switched out because he hadn't done the smallest task of getting his guys together for his lineup. The wedding coordinator was my aunt, and anyone that has worked with her knows that things are done with excellence; she DOES NOT play around. Things will be done when they are supposed to be done, or you will be replaced, and that's pretty much what had to happen, which caused a lot of stress. Some say that I was a Bridezilla, and I probably was. The wedding party was huge. It had to be. I alone had three sides of family that had to be represented, and he had two, and I made absolutely sure that there was someone from each side. I ended up with a total of about 15 Brides Maids, including the Matron and Maids of Honor, so that meant he had 15 Groomsmen, including his Best Man. The wedding was almost perfect, but we had a few kinks here and there, but it didn't matter. We had overcome the obstacles thrown at us, and we were now one. Mr. and Mrs.

English, Jr. It had been a long time coming, and now, I just wanted to rest in it. I had fought hard to prove my love and loyalty. We really didn't have a honeymoon because we both wanted to get back to work. We did, however, take about three days away, with just he and I. I wish it could have been more because we knew we still had a journey ahead of us.

We had to wait a few weeks before we were able to move into our new place as husband and wife. When we were able to move in, we were so excited. It was a little way out, so no one would just pop up without us being aware, and it was kind of a quiet neighborhood. The time was still new for us as we were just beginning to settle in, but we did have family that came through and spent time with us. We had the kids every other weekend, so we had a room for them, and we prepared it for them. Things were good, as we all were still trying to adjust to us all being together under one roof. It was an apartment, but it was perfect for us. We had two bedrooms and 1 ½ baths, and the master had a walk-in closet. For those that know me, you know I was in paradise. We made it ours. Even though we were in our new home and in a new season in our lives, there was still something that we had to face, no matter where we were and no matter how good things seemed to be.

It was our time to be alone, as the boys were with their mother this particular weekend. We had planned a date night where we were just going to enjoy each other and enjoy being alone. Babe had cooked, and we just sat down to enjoy the evening. Before we could even get started, the phone rang. No guess of who it was on the other line. "Babe, give me a minute to talk to her and see what's going on." No response was given, just a look, and those that know me for real, know that my looks can be deadly. I already knew how the night was going to end. My husband gets up from the couch and walks from the living room to our bedroom to talk to his ex-wife because she is in one of her moods and feels like having a fit this particular day. What was supposed to take a few minutes took the entire rest of the night. I woke up on the couch the next morning, alone. You can probably guess that I was not a happy camper and really didn't know how to express my feelings. At this point, the 20-minute agreement was out the door. Yes, I was upset and hurt because, as it was before we got married, here we are, still dealing with issues that are no longer our concern. This was the first time in our marriage where what the ex-wife needed, or wanted, took precedence over me, his current wife. No matter how much my husband tried to get me to see that it was for the sake of the kids that he was putting up with the foolishness, I did not see it. What I saw as a woman was another woman using her power as the mother of his children to get what she wanted, and the major excuse for the allowance of the behavior was, "It's for my kids." This being the first of many to come, it created discord in our home and our relationship. There had already been ill feelings planted in the kids' heads against me, so it was hard to build on top of that. They were told by their dad to be kind, to be respectful, etc., and they were, as they are really good boys. However, when we were together, there was a lot of tension all the time.

At this time, I was working 12-hour shifts, 3 days per week, about 30-45 minutes away. By the time I got home, I was drained, exhausted, and really didn't feel like doing anything. That meant cooking, cleaning, and anything. I would just want to get out of my scrubs, shower, and relax. Of course, being a wife and now stepmother, it didn't happen like that. With the foolishness that was going on with the calls all the time and pretty much being pushed aside, on top of the long days, I didn't want to have to come home to a sink full of dishes or having to clean the bathroom, etc. I selfishly made the statement, "I work 12-hour days with sick people that I have to clean up after, and I don't want to have to come home and do the same thing." It didn't turn out well, and it caused more discord and argument. Well, this was a learning experience because it was a prime example of not having to say everything that comes to mind.

With this being my first marriage and it being his second, I knew there were a lot of things that I didn't know and would have to learn. I also felt like I should be able to learn from him as well, being that he had already been married before. To him, it was like a new thing, like he hadn't been married before. I only wished that that were true in all aspects of our lives. I was open to doing whatever I needed to do as a wife to make my husband happy. That did not include being disrespected or taking foolishness from his ex-wife. He would always say that he never wanted me to have to deal with what he had to endure with her, so he would take it all to protect me from it. I never wanted him to do that. I always wanted us to be able to discuss it and work through it together. I never wanted him to feel like he had to handle or do anything by himself because he wasn't by himself. When we were dating, my main goal was to be there for him and never to treat him or his family through any unnecessary drama because I already knew the extent of what they had to deal with daily. We had initially discussed that we would communicate about everything so that way, there would be nothing that could catch us by surprise. I already saw the games that were coming and tried to let him know, but of course, he didn't see it that way. I was just being paranoid, according to him. I tried to explain to him that as a woman, I know the games that we play to get what we want or to try to keep communication with someone or something that we don't want to let go of or move away from. We'll do anything just to be close to them again or just to hear their voice again. No matter what I said, it just didn't mean anything. All the phones were in my name. It was mine, his, and his oldest son's. We got his oldest son one while we were dating so that he and his father could communicate when they were not with us, and he wouldn't have to go through her to talk to him. Once she saw that the phone was in my name, she had a fit and told him to come and get it because her son would not be using it. I had already advised him what was going to happen with her, but of course, he didn't believe me. For the sake of keeping peace with my husband, I didn't say much about her acting out. Although I didn't, he knew how I felt about it. After so much disrespect and disregard for me and our relationship/marriage, I would then say something to him. As stated before, all I ever wanted to do was be at peace with him as well as his family, despite the fact that she continued to provoke them.

Even though I wanted to be his and have peace in our relationship, it did not last. Also, as previously stated, I could see the games and the tactics being used to keep division going with me and my husband. Every year, I repeated the same things over and over about how I was not playing this game with the two of them. I let him know that he needed to make a choice of what it was and who it was that he wanted because I refused to live my life going back and forth with the two of them. In words, my husband made it clear who he wanted, but his actions always showed something otherwise.

One night, while still in school pursuing my Medical Assisting Degree, I was headed to school for exams. So, I decided to stop by the church first to see him since the shop was right down the street from the church. As I'm walking in, I notice him and her having a very deep discussion. I said something, walked past them and went to sit down in the shop with the boys. I sat for a few minutes with disgust on my face because I already knew there was going to be some drama. I heard her fussing, but him not really saying anything back, so I got up and went out and asked what the problem was and what was going on. The conversation was not about his sons, so I asked why they were even talking and why she was there. To my surprise, she revealed that they had been talking for two months after we got married. Heat rushed through my body like a surge of some kind of power. "Unless it's about the boys, then you two really shouldn't be talking to each other and really should not have anything to discuss," I said. She laughed and replied, "That's funny because I remember telling you the same thing." I wasn't going back and forth with her or him at that point. I advised him to finish his conversation and let that be the end of it. I went to school, took my exam, left school, went home and packed a bag, and went to stay at my oldest brother's house for the night. I wasn't taking any calls for the rest of the night because I had nothing to say to him. Clearly, he had been lying to me for months. Of course, he called and called, and I didn't answer. He tracked my phone to find out where I was, but I turned my phone off because I was too heated to discuss anything with him. This was the first time I had packed to get away from him, but certainly not the last. I wanted to trust my husband and what he was saying to me from that point on, but it was hard to do because of the numerous instances he had already been dishonest. Even though I had taken my night away, I refused to leave him because we had already invested too much time and because I loved my husband and meant every word of our vows; to be with him through the good and the bad.

Of course, there were other instances of dealing with her and of being disrespected. And even in all of this, I stayed. I stayed, I prayed, I cried, prayed some more, and even had someone that I thought I could confide in. It's definitely true what people say about not involving others in your marriage. There's a whole list of things that can be said about how it hurts the marriage and also causes issues. Now, even though the two of them were over, and we were together, it never seemed like it. She was always around. I know that she is and will always be considered family, but some boundaries should be set and put in place. There were NONE. You can't keep people out of the House of the Lord, but how I wished that she was banned from coming. It seemed that every time she came, it was to cause drama. Now, she is not the kind of person that can come in, blend in, and flow with things; she is the kind that has to be heard, and trust me, everyone knew when she was in the room. It was horrible; it was like the entire atmosphere changed when she came around. Everyone reverted to walking on eggshells and having to watch what they say and do because they didn't want to say anything to upset her. When she was still a member, the service had to be interrupted to pray for her because she got into one of her moods. Even when the Pastor did the introductions, instead of mentioning everyone, they would only mention the kids and grandkids, or I wouldn't be mentioned. Now, of course, I knew what it was for, but that didn't make it hurt any less, and that didn't make it any more disrespectful to me. There were times when I would be introduced or mentioned as a part of the first family, but if I was, then she had to be mentioned as well, so she wouldn't feel a certain way. That became very irritating to me because it showed that they cared more about how she felt and how it was going to affect her, but not me. Yes, I would occasionally bring it up to my husband, but he would always come up with some sad and stupid reason to justify his foolishness. It seemed like he was always standing up for her and her behavior rather than standing up for and defending me. "What do you want me to do, or what do you want me to say? I don't control what my parents do." It became very clear to me that it was always going to be a battle. As with everything else, it was always, "It's for my kids." At times, I would just shake my head and walk away. It had gotten to the point where I didn't and wouldn't come around because I knew she'd be there, and I didn't want to be in the same room with her and be made to feel irrelevant when my feelings should have been most important. Sure, I understood that she was the boys' mother and always would be, but that was no excuse for the things that were allowed to happen or for the things that she was allowed to say. To me, it just felt like they were so comfortable with the control, the chaos, and whatever was "hers."

For years, I prayed that her heart and mind would be healed and the heart and minds of those connected to her. I wanted it to be so that we would be able to be civil to each other because of the kids, but it just never worked that way when I attempted it, but when she attempted it, everyone was just so gung-ho for it. All I could do was shake my head. I started to get phone calls to come to meet so that we could talk, and then about every six months or so, I would get an email, disguised as a prayer, but to really "tell me about myself." There were times that I would meet her without letting him know, and times that I would let him know and not go meet, as he didn't feel it was necessary. However, I began to see that he didn't want us to meet up because he didn't want us talking to each other, as the truth about them would be revealed. There was a time when I told him that I had gone to meet with her, and he became upset. When I told him what we talked about, he, of course, defended her. "You shouldn't have gone to talk to her." "What do you want me to do or say?" My response was, "Nothing, I suppose because you never do." I also then began to see that he was intimidated by her. Whenever we were around her, he would disappear. Or whenever she called, and I was around, he would become this little boy that's afraid of what she will say or how she would act.

One day, while riding in the car with him and the boys, she called, and he barely answered. She sensed he was around someone that wouldn't allow him to talk to her like he normally did if he wasn't around me, and she stated, "What's the problem? I mean, are you around someone, and you can't talk to me?" At that point, I knew that they had been having other conversations that they should not have. Yes, I noticed and heard a lot that I never said anything about, but that never meant that I wasn't paying attention. With all the discord that was going on in our relationship, I began to harden my heart and just plan to hate her. Why? You ask? I began to hate her because she knew exactly what she was doing. However, my husband never saw it that way. It was always me making her an issue when he claimed that she was not. With me feeling this way, I suggested to him that he return to her to reunite his family. It seemed like he had a mix-up about who he was married to.

Another instance of her being defended as if he was still married to her and not to me. The baby boy had been having headaches, and one particular Sunday, he had a really bad one, so they took him to the emergency room. It was later detected that he had something serious going on in his head and that he would need surgery, so he had to be admitted. No problem, we're going to the hospital, and we were going to be by his side. What happened next changed the entire trajectory of our marriage from that point on. My husband said, "I need you to stay home. I will keep you posted. Excuse me! Let me go and be with my son and figure out what's going on." Yes, this is what MY husband said to me, his wife. "So, bottom line, you want me to stay in this house alone while you're at the hospital with your ex-wife and son. I couldn't believe my freaking ears." One night turned into a couple of weeks of him coming to get clothes and staying at the hospital with his son and ex-wife. Oh, but wait, it gets better. I, his wife, was not permitted to visit the hospital or see the baby boy without her permission and without him first consulting with her. My husband had to give me, his wife, permission to visit my stepson in the hospital. Where do they do that at????? Please tell me. After that visit, my husband and I had a very serious discussion, and I told him exactly how I felt, and it wasn't pretty. This person is allowed to wreck and run our lives completely, and everyone is cool with that. This was the last straw. I had had enough!!! My husband spent the night at the hospital, leaving me alone again. So, what does this look like to me? Clearly, you want to be with your ex-wife and children because their needs are more important than ours. When I got home, I packed my belongings and left the next day. I called my sister and told her I was on my way. I had inquired about jobs and was ready to send my resume because I had made up my mind that I was not going to put up with this nonsense any longer, and I wanted to be as far away from him and her as possible. I was heartbroken. Who marries to be divorced or treated as if they don't matter? I meant every word when I said I wasn't going to play the back-and-forth game with them, but at the same time, and on the same token, I loved my husband. I was never the same after that. Our marriage was never the same after that. I didn't want to speak to or see him. Yes, he was upset because I had abandoned him without informing him, but why did he need an explanation? He had shown me everything I needed to see. He came to get me back and pretty much told me that I was not leaving him. We talked, but I didn't go back just yet. I probably stayed away for about 6-8 months before moving back in with him. I wasn't going back to the same behavior. If he was going to continue to defend her and put her needs above ours, there was no use thinking about going back. Things were different for a while, or so I thought. We had discussions about finance and how things were sorted with the two of them as it pertained to the kids. I didn't hear much from her, but that doesn't mean that he didn't. He always said that he would just take it all from her so that I didn't have to deal with it, but I hated when he said that because there were some things that he should not have been dealing with from her, period. The way I see it was that she only did what they allowed her to do, and I mean, just about everyone allowed it. And you can guess it. "It's for the kids." It was so bad that the kids knew they couldn't say or do some things when their mother was around because it might set her off.

My relationship with the kids was very strained. They had been trained and told not to like me. It had pretty much been pumped into their heads that I was the reason that their mom and dad were not together anymore. The boys were good boys and wanted peace with everyone, but it was really naïve to think that there would be peace. That's what we all wanted, but that's never what we got. Things could be fine, and then one day, out of the blue, she's calling, in one of her moods, crying about everything that had been done to her for the last ten years, with dates and times of the events. It was hard for everyone involved, especially the kids. Where I wanted to be a part of their lives, I really couldn't because of what had been pumped into their heads, and also because it was like, them (him and the boys) and then me. There was always a wedge there. Please don't get me wrong or misunderstand me in any way, these are two of the sweetest, well-mannered boys ever, but they also had times that they plotted and planned for it to just be them and their dad, and it was fine with him. I pretty much got to a place where I did everything on my own. They would be in either their room with him or the living room with him, and I would be in my room doing my own thing.

Now, anyone who knows me knows that I love kids and want my own kids someday. But because of the medical condition, I'm not able to have kids right now. It has gotten to the point where getting pregnant and carrying a child to term is almost non-existent for me. The process and the space that the baby requires would be harmful to my breathing and could kill my baby or me. This is what a Pulmonary Specialist told me. Hearing that really broke my heart, and it has been something that I struggle with every day. I discussed it with my husband, and he pretty much told me that he didn't want me to have a baby. First, he said that he wouldn't want anything to happen to me, and he didn't want to be put in a place of having to choose between his wife and his baby, but it then came out that he didn't want me to have a baby because it would pretty much take me away from him. Once again, I couldn't believe what I was hearing. You don't want me to have a baby because I would do to you what you've pretty much done to me our entire relationship/marriage?? How could he be so selfish?? That was yet another thing that has stuck with and pushed me away even more. By this time, I'd pretty much checked out. I mean, I'm there, but I'm not. I'm still trying to be there and to be present, but it was becoming more difficult to do so. There were times that I would get frustrated with him and the kids. When they came to us, it was like a newfound freedom for them. They were able to relax and pretty much do whatever they wanted to do. I hated washing dishes, and

I actually still do. I was so happy that at our current residence, we had a dishwasher. It was a pet peeve of mine for dishes to be left in the sink with food and condiments still on them. I felt like if you're going to leave it for someone else to clean, at least rinse it off completely. I also felt that the boys were old enough to clean up after themselves. I knew that they had chores at home, so why should it be any different at our home? We never imposed chores on them, but I did expect them to clean up after themselves. I felt like if they were old enough and smart enough to have iPhones and tablets, then they were old enough to wash their dishes and clean up their messes. Well, of course, my husband didn't agree and only enforced it when it was coming from him to do. Then, on the other hand, when they saw a dish of mine in the sink or on the counter, he would get frustrated and upset with me because why should they have to do it if I wasn't? Because I was going to be the one to clean and wash them anyway, I figured I would get them on my own time and do it all at once. Things had just gotten different. It got to the point where I started sleeping on the couch. I would rather be on the couch alone than in bed with him. It wasn't that I didn't love him or didn't want to be with him, it was just that so much had transpired, and we were just in a place of, "what for?" It got to the point where we were more like roommates than husband and wife.

With everything else being so weird with us, our intimacy was no different. Again, something was just off and not right. My mind was flooded with so many different things that could have been causing this feeling. Neither of us could really figure out what was going on, so we blamed it on the medicines we were taking and how they could have been affecting us and causing changes in mood, hormones, etc. My husband had gotten sick and had to go to the ER. I always ensured he was taking his medications. While at the ER waiting for the doctor to come in, we were talking and really just trying to figure out what was happening and why. Every time I went over to my husband to check on him, his blood pressure would shoot up. It wasn't making sense to me. Something else was going on that he wasn't telling me about. I then started having people coming up to me in church, praying for me and him, and pretty much telling me that I wasn't doing enough as his wife, that I needed to step it up, and that I needed to forgive him and let it go, and let God heal us and our relationship. I would give him the death stare as if to say, "what are you telling them, and what are they talking about?"

It was probably a week or two after that day that I went

to see my husband at work while he was cleaning up to end the day. Now, I had always told my husband that if either of us cheated, we'd be able to talk about it as husband and wife and work through it. If you're going to cheat, there's no reason for us to be together, in my opinion. My words were being thrown back at me this night. It was positioned like, you said this, so let's see how true that was and if you stand by what you said. My husband then confessed to me that he had cheated on me. What I was hearing was completely unbelievable to me. Here we go again with some nonsense. We talked for a few more minutes before I got up to leave. I didn't want to talk about it anymore, and I didn't want to be in his presence anymore. It was a couch night for me.

The Pastor approached me the following Sunday, and he told me the same thing. My husband had cheated, and now there was a meeting with the Elders of the church to discuss it. I discovered that many people already knew what was going on and what had happened. Hurt, pissed, embarrassed, and humiliated were all the things that I was at that current moment. My husband most certainly downplayed the incident. During the meeting, I discovered that this had occurred four months prior to my discovery. At this point, I was ready to crack a scull or two. My husband had pretty much been looking at me every single day, lying to my face, for FOUR MONTHS!!! It was easy for me to get past the fact that he had done it, and even who he had done it with, but the fact that he had been lying to me for four months???? Yeah, I really checked the freak out from that point on. Now it was all making sense. No wonder his freaking pressure kept shooting up when he was in the ER. He was lying and keeping secrets, and they were making him sick. He just knew in his mind that if and when he told me, I was going to leave him. At this point, I realized that he had no intention of telling me what had happened. He only told me because his parents knew and had threatened him that if he didn't tell me, they were going to. That made it even worse.

Everything was really becoming crystal clear. No wonder the girl he cheated with was saying certain things. No wonder she would hang around the shop even when I offered her a ride home. No wonder she was staring at me as if she wanted to kill me. I mean, seriously, the spirit was so high during worship service one Sunday, and my feet got light, and this girl tapped in. When I got myself together and opened my eyes, this girl was staring me dead in my face like she wanted me to drop dead right then and there. I really didn't pay much attention to it or tell him because everyone knew that this girl was off, but it all made sense.

As time went by, more pieces to the story started to be revealed. The crazy girl even started posting pictures of herself being pregnant and about her boo coming over and her cooking for him. It was funny because I knew that was a lie, all of it. It was bad because the girl had done my hair a few times, and we had discussed some personal things, one being how neither of us could have kids because of the situations we were facing and the conditions that we had to deal with. I congratulated her on being pregnant, if she was, especially since I knew that was a desire for her. I sent the picture to my husband and pretty much told him that if the girl was pregnant, and if it was his, we were done, and I meant every word of that.

In the meeting at the church with all the leaders of the church, I was advised that I could walk away from the marriage because there were grounds for me to do so now. Yeah, I knew that that's what a lot of people wanted, and that was okay, but that's not the choice we made. Although we decided to stay together and work through it, things were still never going to be the same. I no longer had any trust in or for my husband. If he could look me in my face for four months and lie to me, then that pretty much said a lot that he didn't love and respect me the way he claimed to. Of course, with bits and pieces still coming out of the story, I discovered that what had happened was not the first time it had happened. There had been instances that led to that one. That made me even more upset and so ready to be completely done with him. The entire situation could have been avoided and even handled if he had told me what he had done from the start. Instead of him telling me, he decided that he could handle it himself, and it continued to happen. This caused so many arguments between us. He wanted things to go back to how they were, but it was never going to be that. For four months, he lied to me about everything. He wasn't even going to tell me. He had been intimate with this girl, and then came home to me, and wanted to, and was intimate with me. Again, that weird feeling began to make so much sense. It wasn't me; it was him and his dealings causing this weird aura between us.

Of course, to him, I was just supposed to pick up and move on like nothing ever happened. He felt that since he had confessed and I decided to stay with him and work through it, things were just supposed to go back to normal. NO!!!! He was wrong. Through all of this, I had seen that I had pretty much settled for all the foolishness and pretty much everything that I allowed to happen.

Some time passed, and we were moved from the townhouse to our new house. We had pretty much ended our lease and had given our home to another family. We packed up and put our things in storage and stayed with his parents until our home was ready for us to move in. At this time, my condition had begun to manifest itself. I already had trouble breathing, and exertion made it worse. It had gotten so bad that when I coughed, my entire body was in so much pain. Everyone could see the pain that I was in, and they all made me go to the ER. I was having chest pain and back pain around the kidney area, and it was pretty much hurting me and taking the wind out of me to use the restroom. I know I sat and waited for a very long time after being triaged. I watched people walk in and out and watched people that had come in after me being roomed before me. My sister went to the front to find out what was going on and to let them know that they needed to speed it up and get me in a room because of what was going on with me. The Patient Access Rep asked, "Is she dying? If not, then she's going to have to wait." My sister confronted the rep and informed him that I was having chest pains. At that point, they decided that they wanted to do something and sent a nurse back to do an EKG. After the EKG, they began to speed things up and got me in a room immediately. This made me know something was happening that they didn't mention to me. Based on my EKG and all the symptoms I was having, I was admitted. I had never been admitted to a hospital in my 38 years of life. I found out later that the Sarcoidosis had spread from my lungs to my heart, causing me to have Pulmonary Hypertension, which basically means high blood pressure in my lungs. I was hospitalized for five days. Because I had never been admitted to the hospital before, and because of the severity of my condition, it was a terrifying time for everyone who was close to me. My husband was there with me for a few days in the hospital, but not all day, and he probably stayed one night out of the five. Yes, that bothered me because when the baby boy was in the hospital, he was there every single day and stayed every single night. I didn't mention it, though. For the most part, my mom was there with me every day. My sister stayed a couple of nights, and my mom stayed a couple of nights. The only night he stayed with me was the day I wanted mom to go home and get some rest.

These five days changed everything in my life. I had been

looking for jobs and had applied and interviewed with so many places. While I was in the hospital, about three jobs were offered to me, and I couldn't take any of them. The doctors had taken me off of work, so that meant a change for my household. Now, he was the only one bringing in money. I had to apply for financial assistance and also applied to Medicaid, as well as Medicare. The doctors didn't want me working because the jobs that I had interviewed for and my previous jobs were on the phone. Well, it was difficult for me to talk for long periods of time, so I couldn't continue as a customer service rep, nor could I really do anything that required too much movement, walking, bending, etc.

With no money coming in from me, that put more of a strain on our relationship, and now he pretty much had to take care of me. That's not really something that he wanted to do. He had already told me that if something were to happen that left me incapacitated or where he wouldn't be able to take care of me; he would put me in a nursing home. I was hurt by that statement, but I kept going. True intentions were being revealed. While all of this was going on, we were almost to the point where the house would be ready for us. We were talking about the rooms, who would have what, and where. My husband wanted to convert the then-master bedroom into a studio/mancave for him and put me on the other side of the house in a smaller room that required me to go upstairs to access it. This caused confusion because, once again, I felt he was being selfish, and I expressed my concerns to him. The master bedroom was on the main level, near the kitchen, the washer, and the dryer, and it also had a bathroom. It just made more sense for us to have that as our bedroom because it was more convenient for me health-wise, especially being able to wash clothes, cook, and use the restroom without having to go up or down steps. We were talking about it before I had to go to the ER and was admitted.

I had to go up the steps to get to our then bedroom, and when I walked up the steps, I held my breath, which caused me to have a high heart rate, and caused a coughing fit. On one of those days, as I was walking up the stairs, I heard my father-in-law say, "She didn't have a problem going up the steps then, did she, son?" And they both laughed. When I came back down the stairs with what I went up for, I was panting for air and out of breath. I didn't say anything at the time, but I told him how I felt about my health being used as a joke before the night was over. "Honey, we would never joke about your health." "Well, honey, you both just did," I replied and walked away. There was still some disagreement about the master room, but it eventually became our bedroom. As a result, the three upstairs bedrooms became the man cave and the boys' rooms. Again, it had been largely divided between them and me, but I stayed in my room a lot. I had everything I needed in that room; a tv, fridge, restroom, and the kitchen a few steps away.

Although I was home, I still had to fight mentally to hold it together. I attempted so hard not to lose my faith and to keep trusting and believing in God. On the outside, I was still smiling and looking like I was okay, minus the oxygen tank. I had to have oxygen tanks and concentrators and had to wear oxygen throughout the day. I was on so many medications, most of which affected my weight, mood, and generally everything about me. I was on medications that made me hallucinate and then some that made me a complete basket case. There were some moments, days, and weeks when I was so depressed by everything, but I couldn't share it. With all that was going on with us in our marriage, and me feeling like I was having to compete with so many things and people for time with my husband, on top of the country entering the COVID-19 pandemic, and being in isolation, I was really started to lose it. I had days that I locked myself in my room, and I would go in the bathroom and just cry, but I never wanted my husband to see me in those moments. I was so depressed and even had thoughts of suicide many days, but I held on to my faith and the word of the Lord. I had to have music to get me through. I had to have worship music. I couldn't go to church, and my husband would work all day and then come home worn out and too tired to really do anything. It was during this time that we grew further apart.

Despite all that had transpired between us, I still loved my husband and wanted us to work. I felt like he was being insensitive to my feelings, and he felt the same way. No matter what happened, we just didn't see things eye to eye. With the door to our room locked, I would go into the bathroom, shut the door, sit on the edge of the tub and just cry. Dealing with the condition, being isolated, and dealing with the ups and downs of marriage were just overwhelming all at once, and I felt like my husband just didn't love me. Yeah, he said it out of his mouth, but I always questioned whether it was true and if he meant it. There could be no way that he loved me and everything and everyone else would be a priority, but not me. There were days when I didn't want to get out of bed, and most of those days, I didn't. There were days that I would be there alone, all day, practically every day, and I would get up for a few hours, mess around with some things, and then get back in bed. One of the medicines had caused insomnia, so my schedule was completely different from his. He was up all day, and I would be up all night. We were distant and had been that way for some time now, but this was the worst and the longest it had ever been.

The holidays had rolled around, and I still felt the same way. I didn't really want to be bothered by anyone or with anyone. I really hadn't even planned on leaving the house for Christmas. My husband and I had a disagreement about what had happened earlier that morning. We eventually got that resolved and had plenty of time to listen and hear each other. Later, I was informed that his mother wanted everyone to come to the house. I had no intention of going anywhere because I was used to being alone and spending the day at home by myself, and today was no exception. I knew something was going on because my husband had been dropped off. The second thing that made me wonder how the rest of the day was going to go was that when we left the house, we weren't going to his parents' house. Instead, we were on our way to pick up the boys. I questioned that in my head because, once again, I suspected something was wrong. I couldn't figure out why we were coming to pick them up, and I knew the oldest son owned a car and could have driven himself there. We all arrived at his parents' house, and everyone immediately went their separate ways when we entered. I went to the living room and sat down on the couch, but almost everyone else was in the kitchen and dining rooms. Dad came to sit and talk to me, but that was it. A few minutes later, I see everyone walking out to the garage with so much excitement. I stayed where I was, but my husband said, "Come on, Cho." I'm looking at him like, for what? I get outside to the garage, and there is an Escalade Truck in the garage, and my husband is handing his oldest son the keys, and they're hugging each other. "Merry Christmas, son; I'm so proud of you. I love you, man." "Thanks, dad," the oldest said with so much satisfaction on his face. I was looking around the room, and it was clear to me that everyone else was already aware of what had just happened. I looked at my husband in disgust and just walked away. Again, the fury and the feeling in my soul were unspeakable. I was on fire! Okay, so you may be thinking, why am I mad about him buying his son a car? It wasn't the fact of him buying the car for his son because we had discussed getting a car for him when he graduated and was headed to college. The issue was that he never mentioned it to me, not one time. He had had the car for a whole week, parked at the shop, and still never mentioned it to me. He had the whole thing planned out and never mentioned it to me at all. The second thing was, I know he had discussed it with the ex-wife, but he NEVER mentioned it to me at all. I'm really looking at him like I could kill him because he planned and did something without talking to me, his wife, and I'm looking clueless, and his family is looking at me like, why does she have an attitude?

I had nothing to say for the rest of the time in the house, I had nothing to say on the ride home, and when I got home, I went straight to the room and shut the door. After about 20 minutes or so, he came into the room to find out what was going on and why I didn't have anything to say to him. There was already tension between us because we hadn't talked in about two to three days. We were both sitting on the side of the bed calmly. We began discussing the events of the day, and somehow the car got left out. So, I said, "You know you were wrong." "How was I wrong, and what was I wrong about," he replied. I proceeded to tell him that he was wrong about the car and how he handled the entire situation. Now, anytime I mentioned the boys, regardless of what it was for, he would jump on the defensive like he was talking to someone who was intentionally trying to cause harm to them, not like I was his wife. I attempted to further explain that it's a problem when I ask him for anything financially, which is why I never would. The only thing that he would buy for me would be food, and he even had a problem with that. So, I asked him to explain how he could so willingly buy his newly graduated, 17-year-old, soon-to-be 18, a car like that, and 1, not mention it to me, and 2, have an issue with doing what he was supposed to do as my husband and provide for me. Then I said, "clearly, you had no issue whatsoever doing anything that was asked of you by your sons and their mother, but you have an issue doing anything for your wife, the one you claimed you love and want to be with." The conversation got heated, and I told him that I was tired of him putting his sons and everyone else before me. He asked me what I said, and I repeated it. He yelled, "My sons will ALWAYS come before you." Oh, that hit a nerve, and my response was, "F*%ck you and your sons." He had a red cup of something in his hand that he was drinking, and he threw the whole cup in my face. Whatever he was drinking was red, and it got all over me, the bed, my hair, the nightstand, and the wall. He was heated and pretty much yelling and cussing me out at that point. Even with all of that, I stayed calm and tried to talk to and reason with him, but he was not having it or hearing it. He continues with, "You ain't shit, your family ain't shit! You lay in that bed every day and do nothing! I fucking hate you!" By this time, I was heated, and we were in each others' faces, and when he told me that he hated me, that was it. I tried to hit him in the face, but he stopped me and threw me into the closet door. I fell to the floor and blacked out for a couple of seconds, tried to regain myself, and went towards him again. This time he pushed me into the wall again, and I hit my head and blacked out again. I tried to get back up but was out of breath and coughing really badly, and on all fours, crawling on the floor to regain my breath. He pretty much watched me crawling on the floor. I got up again and went after him one more time, and this time, he grabbed me and pinned me up against the wall and yelled, "DON'T F*%CK WITH ME!" By this time, my head began to start pounding, and I felt a knot on the back of my head that was getting bigger by the moment. After the last pin-up, he walked away and called the police, and also texted my sister to come and get me out of HIS house. "Come and get her a** now! She got to get the f*%ck out of here, the text said. I called my mom and told her to come and get me. I told her what had happened and that she would have to take me to the ER because my head was hurting.

I was trying not to hear anything when the police came in and said their spill. I gathered my belongings and left for the hospital. While at the hospital, I had to explain what had happened, and they performed an examination. They provided me with information on domestic violence. When I looked at and read all the information, I realized I was in a domestic violence situation. Everything on the list was something I had experienced with him: isolation, intimidation, denial, and blaming, as well as emotional and financial abuse. Those were all things that I had experienced with him. I know that some of it may have been caused by how he was treated in his previous marriage, but he was now doing to me what had been done to him.

The doctor measured the knot on my head to be about three centimeters. I went down to file a restraining order against him after leaving the ER. Even in the midst of everything that was going on and had happened, he was still my husband. I knew he wasn't abusive, physically because this was the first time in our entire marriage that we had ever had an altercation like this that resulted in violence. I didn't want to put him out of his own house, but it was clear that we could not be around each other for the next 5-7 days. I just decided to go to the house, pack a few bags with clothes for the next week, and go to my mom's house. We had not talked for the rest of that night and the next week. While I was gone, based on the restraining order, he had the locks changed. This was the second time he had done that to me, changing the locks. I hadn't left, and I hadn't moved out, but he still decided to change the locks, and only he and his sons had the new keys.

When the order was over, I attempted to go back to the house to get in, and of course, I couldn't. I attempted reaching out to him to get back in the house, but he wanted to be difficult, and he wouldn't let me in or give me a key. I called the police at that point. When they got there, they told me that there was nothing they could do because he refused to let me back in, but they advised me that since I had established residence at the house for more than three days, I could use any means necessary to get in, whether to break the door down, bust a window, or whatever. I was still thinking rationally, but my family wasn't. We checked all the doors, and they were locked, but my aunt and sister found that my bathroom window was unlocked. Both of them climbed through my bathroom window to open the door. It wasn't open enough for them to get through all the way, so the blinds were damaged, but who cared? What was important was that I had gotten back in the house. After getting in, I made the decision that I wasn't leaving. For the first couple of nights, I slept with a knife in my nightstand drawer. While the police were there with us, they informed me that they were unable to serve him because he was never home. I gave them the shop address and what color his truck was, and they left. As they were leaving, he was coming down the street. They circled back and picked him up to complete the serving of the warrant. He had to ride in the back of the police car downtown, but he was released the same night. When he got back to the house, I was in there. We didn't have anything to say to each other. He went to his cave, and I stayed in mine.

We are both very stubborn, so I could and would go days without saying anything to him and be okay. I could pretty much make it as though he was invisible, as again, I was so used to and comfortable with being alone and doing things on my own. After a few days, we finally broke down and said something to each other. We had a discussion about everything that had transpired, from Christmas day and beyond. What was really baffling to me was that I knew his parents had heard what had happened, but I didn't hear anything from them. On 10/26, I called his dad, talked to him, and told him what happened because I knew that he hadn't been told the truth. When I told him what had happened, he was shocked and apologetic because that was not what his son had told him. They thought I was aware of the car, and he told them that I was okay and didn't need to go to the ER because nothing was wrong with me. Of course, he made it seem like I always had an attitude for nothing, but he never explained why I was upset or had an attitude. He would never tell them the truth of the matter or reveal what was really going on. Yes, I know that I have a very strong attitude, and sometimes I can be a beast and maybe even a witch with a B, but it was definitely for a reason. I already knew that I was going to be portrayed as the bad wife, and I dealt with it. I dealt with it because I knew what was really going on in our household, and they only knew what they were told.

At this point, I was so beyond everything. I was tired of arguing, fighting, having to prove myself to him and them, and dealing with not being a priority to my husband. I finally decided to leave for good, but it was going to be over a span of time. This would be a meticulous move—one that was planned out and one that would be a lasting decision. I ended up moving out in March of 2021. I had no intention of coming back or even being with him anymore. It was the best decision I had made for myself at the time. The stress, the arguing, and fighting were stressing me out even more and definitely played a major part in my health and the condition I was facing.

Walking away from a life of being controlled by his ex-wife brought <u>me</u> so much peace to me. I had lost some weight, and everyone kept telling me that I looked good and healthy and that I was glowing. I was even able to come off some of the medications. For a while, I was good. He and I were still communicating every now and then, but not often. It had become apparent that the ex-wife was around and at the house more and more. When we did speak to each other, I, of course, asked what was going on. It was baffling to me because they don't get along. As everyone was always quick to say, it's a difficult situation. I had my own feelings about it, but it wasn't even worth expressing anymore at this point. He preceded to tell me that his sons had moved in with him. All I could do was laugh because I know how we women think. When we were together, there would have been no way she would have allowed that, but I saw it as proof that she knew exactly what she was doing. His wife is no longer there, so I'll give him what he wants (his boys), and that will allow me to be closer to him. It was at this point of talking to him that I realized and began to see that he still didn't understand why I left and that he probably didn't care because he had what he cared most about, his boys. That day, I blocked him completely from everything: no calls, no texts, and no social media platforms. I had seen that nothing had changed, so I knew that they never would.

Now divorce was on my mind more than ever. I started researching different filing options. At first, it had crossed my mind to be petty and seek spousal support. Why wouldn't I, and why shouldn't I? He vowed to take care of me, and he didn't hold true to that vow. The way I looked at it was that he chose to put the needs and wants of others before mine and ours, so he owed me.

What I saw in myself was something of the flesh. I wanted vengeance, knowing it does not belong to me, for vengeance is mine saith the Lord, Rom. 12:19. I got involved with Bible Study groups, self-confidence courses, master classes, and challenges. I began studying the Word more and praying more, and in this, God began to send me signs and confirmations. One of the clearest things that I heard Him speak to me was, "Let it go. I will restore." That hit my spirit so hard, and I immediately started crying and thanking Him for confirmation and assurance. I was at peace with what I heard and knew it was the voice of the Lord. While in my waiting period, I continued working on myself. I would always look back to see what I could have done differently and what was hurting in me that needed to be addressed and that I needed to be healed of. I knew that I had to forgive myself first, then forgive him for not being what I wanted and needed him to be to and for me.

In no way am I saying that he is a bad person because that would be a total lie. And in no way am I saying that I did everything right because I didn't, and I know that life is filled with lessons daily to be taught and learned. I also realized in this that he was hurt and hurting, not just from the things that had transpired with us and within our relationship but before me as well. What it all boiled down to was that we were neither what each of us needed the other to be. Even in all of this, I began to have ill feelings, my heart was jaded, and I began to feel emotions of bitterness. I refused to let that sit in, so I reached out to him. I didn't want to go through life angry, bitter, and hating him. With us starting out as friends, I made a promise that I would always have his best interest at heart and that whether we made it together or not, I would always love him. We met up, and I told him how I felt, and he did the same. We made it clear that we would not be reuniting, but the more we communicated with each other, the more the lines blurred. Even though we were on good terms, I knew the divorce had to be finalized. Again, it was apparent that we were not seeing things eye to eye and even more apparent that we probably never would. I had to again make the best decision for me and maintain my peace. Then, on the other side of things was the thought of wanting to try to work things out. Although my wall of defense was up, I still felt that as long as there is breath in my body, there was still a chance for us to work things out. Even though I know that we can't compare ourselves and our situation to other people and relationships/marriages, I felt that if some of these other relationships out there have made it through their tests and trials, we could. It was clear that we both still loved each other very much and that we didn't want to be with anyone else, but it was also clear that we just didn't agree on some very key things that affected our relationship.

Growing up in the church, we were always taught

against divorce, so even though the filing had already been done, I still felt there was still hope to prevent the completion of the process. I'm sure that it can be figured out, but I'm saying it so that it's clear. I LOVED MY HUSBAND and always will. It should be no secret that this is the case. I have spent 15 years of my life with this man. Who wants to let something like that go? Things were so good when it was just us, but it became a problem when everything and everyone else came into the mix. It would be foolish of me to think that things and people wouldn't be involved, but it still is a wonderful feeling when they're not. When I got the final decree in the mail, I informed him that I had it and that we needed to plan a meeting time to have it signed. It took him by surprise, but I wasn't sure why because we had already discussed this happening. Because we were in communication with one another, he felt I could have let him in sooner than I did. I accepted how he felt, but I still didn't understand it because it was something that had already been discussed.

Once the paperwork was filed with the court, he had 21 days to contest. He chose not to contest, so the paperwork was filed, and the judge signed off on it a few days later. Because we had been through so much already and fought so much before and during our marriage, I just didn't have the strength, energy, or desire to fight anymore. I just wanted things to be as simple as possible for myself and him. All I ever wanted from him was to be loved and to be treated as a woman, his woman, his wife. I didn't request anything from him because all I wanted at this point was to maintain peace. Yes, some may think that's foolish, but I really don't care. Peace is worth so much more than any amount of money. Yes, I could have chosen to be petty and go after him, but that's not what you do to someone you love. God promised me that He would restore, and I trust Him to do just that. He is not a man that He should lie, so I believe what He said.

Once I received my papers from the court, it started sitting in; I am divorced. I'm not going to ask how we got to this point because I'm very much aware of how we got here. It hit me like a ton of bricks. I have cried so much more after the fact than what I did going through it or deciding to do it. I can honestly say that this has felt like I died. I would be at work, minding my business, with my headphones on, and the tears would just start flowing. This is not how it was supposed to be. When I got married, it was a for-life thing. I wanted it to be my first and my only. I also understand that things happen, every action has a reaction, as well as every choice has a consequence, whether it be good or bad. Yes, it hurts, but I trust and believe God to heal every area of my life that has been affected by this breakup and every area of his life.

I don't know what this next chapter will hold for me, but what I do know is that GOD WILL RESTORE! I know that God can and will heal, and this next chapter will be the best one yet. I will continue to work on myself and continue to allow God to make me who He created me to be. Fifteen years is a long time to love someone, so I know it will not be easy to move on. Yes, I endured a lot, but I refuse to close myself or my heart off to love or from being happy. This did affect me in so many different ways, especially emotionally, and it definitely did something to my confidence. However, I love myself, God loves me, and I will continue to work on myself to build myself back up.

God, thank You! Thank You for being Almighty, All-Knowing, and All-Powerful. Thank you for being the Peacekeeper and the Peacemaker. Lord, I am praying for the peace of every woman or man that has been hurt emotionally, physically, and mentally. God, I thank you that you are working on me, in me, and through me, and restoring what was broken. I thank you for every woman/man that is sitting, wondering where their help is coming from, and wondering what move to make next. God, thank you for giving us Your word that is a lamp to our feet and light unto our path. Thank you for giving us wisdom and understanding in all things. Thank you, Lord, for making us new by Your shed blood and by the washing of Your word. Lord, thank You for giving us peace that surpasses all understanding that guides our hearts and minds. God, we come against the spirit of heaviness, bitterness, rejection, fear, abuse, and vengeance. We know that you took everything to the cross of Calvary. We take each of these things and cover them in your blood. Heal us, God, everywhere that we hurt. Allow us to take the hurt and use it as a stepping stone to greater heights. Even when it seems that it's hard, God, help us to see that greater is He that is in us than he who is the world. Help us to see that there are more for us than there are against us. God, heal, restore, mend, and put us back together. Help us to see that this is not the end but that there is more for each of us. God, we thank you for your healing power. We thank you for your grace that kept us, even when we didn't deserve it, God. We thank you, God, for creating a clean heart in us and renewing a right spirit within us. We can't thank you enough for the love that you show and shower on us daily. We can't thank you for being who you are. God, we thank you now and believe that what we have asked will be granted in your name. We count it all done, in Jesus' Name. Amen and Amen.

Scriptures to Consider

Psalms 119:105 – Thy word is a lamp unto my feet and a light unto my path.

Romans 12:19 – Dearly beloved, avenge not yourselves, but rather give place unto wrath; for it is written. Vengeance is mine; I will repay, saith the Lord.

Ephesians 5:26 – That He might sanctify and cleanse it with the washing of water by the word.

1 John 4:4 – Ye are of God, little children, and have overcome them: because greater is he that is in you, than he that is in the world.

What Did You Take Away From This Chapter

Chapter 6:
A Piece of Redemption: Finding Me

Miriam-Webster defines redemption as the act, process, or instance of redeeming. Looking further into the word redeem, I found that it had multiple meanings. The first one that I came across that caught my eye was to buy back or repurchase. The next definition states that redemption means to be free from what distresses or harms. The next and final one that really caught my eye and stuck with me was to change for the better: to reform. Now, all of these caught my eye because they all in some way suggest that there's a comeback of some sort. The situations that we have faced and come through did not take us out. Yes, they did not take you out. Sis, we made it through. That literally means that we are Come Back Kids, as Coach Sophia Ruffin so eloquently puts it.

Never in a million years would I have imagined that any of those situations would befall me as I went through life. We think that because we are children of God, we will never have to go through anything, but I am here to tell you that this is far from the truth. The Bible tells us that the way of a transgressor is hard, meaning that the way of a foolish man is hard, Proverbs 13:15-18. God never intended for us to walk this path called life alone, for He promised us time and time again that HE would never leave us nor forsake us, Deuteronomy 31:8. However, in each phase of life, we may not always realize the promises that have been made to us, and may not know exactly how to reach out and grab the promises that belong to us.

As I look back over each phase and piece of my life, I realize that they were all the making of me. No, I did not, and I still do not understand them all, but one thing I do know is that they have all been necessary for the Cholee that is before you today. Every dad that used a revolving door, every relationship that didn't turn out to be so good, or so beneficial to me, or even for them, every touch that didn't mean me any good, it all still worked out for my good. Yes, it caused some pain. Yes, it caused some tears. Yes, a lot of tears, yes, but it's all alright. Everything that happened caused me to search inside and FIND ME. Finding me has been one of the biggest obstacles in life because I really didn't know who I was. I was searching for the woman that I wanted to be, the woman that people wanted me to be, or the woman I thought I should be based on what I saw others become or pretend to be. After abandonment, rejection, molestation, insecurities, marriage, separation, divorce, suicidal thoughts, and attempts, the biggest question left was. "WHO AM I?" After making a choice to leave my marriage, this was something that I had to constantly ask myself. Even though I didn't want to admit it, I had lost a major part of me for trying to be who he wanted me to be, who his family wanted me to be, and who images and appearances said I should be because I was a part of the family. So when I decided to leave, I had to get back to me and fall in love with who Cholee was all over again. I was Cholee, who loved to accessorize, and I mean accessorize anything. I could wear earrings, a necklace, and a bracelet with a sweat suit and be just as comfortable, but then I would always be told I was doing too much or I didn't have to do all of that. Being told this for 10-15 years, you just go with it. So, when it was just me again, I began to do what I loved to do again: accessorize and personalize.

Also, because it was just me, I had to go back to my more humble beginnings, you know, the downsized version of myself. I returned to such a crowded space, but it was familiar, and it was easy to go back to what was familiar to me—familiar things such as writing, reading, praying, devotions, and worshipping. Yes, I did those things wherever I was, but this place had already been sown with my tears and prayers. I joined prayer groups and Bible study groups because I needed to reconnect to The Source and The Truth. I had people that were praying with me and for me and that refused to let me give up, even when there were days that I wanted to. Each of these things played a major part in me finding me. Even though it was in me, as I said previously, I had lost who I was. Don't get me wrong; I am more than grateful to have had somewhere to even be able to come back to and call home.

In my leaving and returning home, I was determined that I had to take my life back, make a statement, and do something for me that not only spoke to me but also to women out in the world. I'm grateful and beyond blessed for the people that God put in my path at that time to push me into another season in my life and out of the rut that I was in. Besides those that were in my inner circle, he sent two angels that spoke life back into me and pushed me into finding the me that I was supposed to be in that new season. Earlier in the chapters, I mentioned that God gave me a dream, and in that dream, HE told me that HE was giving me peace for my pieces. Well, from that was birthed Piece 2 Peace Boutique. This was my baby. It was a line designed for plus-size women, many of whom suffer from chronic illnesses that cause our weight to fluctuate. I'm all too familiar with the frustration of seeing clothing that catches my eye but isn't available in a size larger than a 1x. At the same time, I also launched a Mary Kay business that also fit right into the brand, and then a few months later, I launched a Paparazzi line that also fit into the brand. For the beauty pieces of the brand, the mission is, was, and will always be to inspire women all over the world that no matter what situations we face, we are beautiful, we are more than enough, we are not our circumstances, and we still choose to live life, conditions and all. Our situations do not define the lives that we live or lead, but WE CHOOSE TO LIVE! WE CHOOSE PEACE! We don't choose to be in pieces, but we choose to be at peace.

While my roles have changed a little over the last couple of years, the brand still remains, and new ventures are underway. Piece 2 Peace will be a name that lives on and rings in the ears of many for years to come. I don't know exactly what God has in store for me and for this brand, but what I do know is that I'm expecting Great Things. I'm not perfect, and not every inch of my story has been told, but hopefully, what has been shared has been something that has touched just one somebody and has impressed upon their hearts in some way. In finding me, I hope that other women are able to find themselves as well and know that if I did it and if I was able to "Come Back," then so can they. I want them to know they have choices and are not alone. Follow peace and pursue it, sis, Psalm 34:14.

God, we thank you for being who you are! We thank you for being the Alpha and the Omega, and we thank You for seeing and knowing all. We thank you, God, for knowing our beginning from our end and for seeing what we can't see. Thank you, Lord, for blocking what the enemy meant for evil. God, we know that we don't deserve the grace that you show to us, but we thank you for granting us new mercies daily. We thank You for making Your grace sufficient for us and Your mercies new every morning. Great is Your faithfulness, Lord. Thank You for Your steadfast love, God. Thank You for being a keeper even when we didn't want to be kept God. Thank you for being a healer when we didn't feel that love could reach that deep down to pick us up again. We can never thank You enough for seeing the best in us when all we can see is the bad, the ugly, the monsters, the grimy, and the treacherous us that we sometimes are. We thank You that Your love covers a multitude of faults, God. More than anything, God, we thank You for Your redeeming love; for your love that says that it's not over and that we can live again. God, we thank you for the power to live again and find us again. With this newfound power, God, help us find ourselves and get to know more of you, the plans that you have for us, and the direction that you would have us go. Help me, God, to use who you have made me to be now to help someone else, and to fulfill your calling for me, God. God, I believe you, and I believe your Word; it shall come to pass on this side, in the land of the living! I claim it, I declare it, and I decree it, in Jesus' matchless name, Amen!

Scriptures to Consider

Proverbs 13:15-18 – [15] Good sense wins favor, but the way of the treacherous never changes. [16] Every sensible person acts knowledgeably, but a fool displays his stupidity. [17] A wicked envoy falls into trouble, but a trustworthy courier brings healing. [18] Poverty and disgrace come to those who ignore discipline, but the one who accepts correction will be honored.

Deuteronomy 31:8 – The Lord is the one who will go before you, He will be with you: he will not leave you or abandon you. Do not be afraid or discouraged.

Psalms 34:14 – Turn away from evil and do what is good; seek peace and pursue it.

What Did You Take Away From This Chapter

Chapter 7:

A Piece of Encouragement: The Best Version of Me

As children, we believe that our parents are telling us the truth and shielding us from things that will harm us. As parents, they take on things that we as children may not understand at an early age because it will break us or because, mentally, we are just not able to comprehend what is really happening. Well, it is the same way with our Heavenly Father. He knows our ending from the beginning and knows what's going to happen step by step, and his goal and will is to protect us from all hurt, harm, and danger. It is when we step outside of that arc of safety that we subject ourselves to the wiles of the devil, his traps, and his snares.

In each piece of my journey, there were times that I stepped outside of the zone of the safety of the Lord, chasing what I wanted and not being in the will of God. It was the prayers of the righteous that sustained and kept me. It was God's plan that I would be able to endure, persevere, and be able to see that strength that I actually possess because of the Greater One who lives on the inside of me. I look back, and all I can do is shake my head and lift my hands, and say, "Thank You, Lord," because Heaven knows that I didn't deserve to make it, but thanks be unto God that His grace is sufficient for me.

The journey told here only details a few of the pieces of the puzzle of Cholee. There are so many more things that I've had to overcome to get to this point in my life, but the things told were a few of the major pieces, and this gives you just a glimpse. My prayer is that within this glimpse, you were able to see some parts of yourself that needed to be spoken to. If so, continue speaking to those parts. Declare each day that the parts that are hidden can be exposed and healed completely. Things that stay in the dark cannot be addressed, nor can they receive healing. Yes, I know that we have always been told that what goes on in our homes stays in our homes, but I bind that devil and demon right now in the name of Jesus. Every spirit of bondage, I come against you with the power of the Blood of Jesus Christ. Every stronghold of the enemy that tries to remain in the dark and hidden, I call it out now, and I decree and declare that WE ARE FREE in the MIGHTY NAME OF JESUS! We will no longer be comfortable keeping secrets and hiding things that are eating away at our very existence. God, YOUR WORD declares that HE whom the SON makes free is free indeed. INDEED, we have been made free by the power of the blood that was shed on the cross of Calvary! That finished work! God, we thank you for the finished work of Calvary! We thank you, God!

Whew, sorry, not sorry. I had to get that out! Ok, so thinking back to the first piece of the puzzle, with the tripod of dads, yes, that looks, sounds, and is dysfunctional, but it's okay. It used to bother me so badly, but I now can look at it as a gift. God loves me so much that he decided to grace me with two sides of family in addition to the two biological sides that I already had. Tell me God is not faithful and just. Tell me that God is not always concerned about me and doesn't know what I need before I do. People may not understand, and people may be confused and joke about it. Remember, people mocked and laughed at Jesus, and HE is the GREATEST MAN I know. I count it an honor to be surrounded by so much love. I also look at it as if I was able to grace them with the privilege of my presence. God made me special, so it's an honor for them to have me and have had me in their lives. The Word of God tells us that iron sharpens iron and also that a child shall lead them. There are definitely times when our fathers need encouragement or when they need a word spoken into their spirits to remind them of the men that they are, and the men that God created them to be. Sometimes as children, we don't understand how our words may affect our parents. Something that we may have spoken to them about may have kept them from making a bad decision or taking a wrong turn. So I encourage each and every one of you to be intentional with your words because they have power. Be intentional with your thoughts because they turn into words or actions. God is intentional in everything that He does, and as He is, so are we, so we must also strive to be intentional in everything that we do, in everything that we say, in the places we go, and in the companies we keep.

One thing I know for sure is that my journey does not end here, for this is only the beginning. This version of me will be the best version of me. I am in a better place with myself, and I am at peace with the things that I have endured. Does that mean that I'm perfect? No. Does that mean that I will forget the things that got me to this point? No. We don't forget the tests and trials that make us stronger, but we forgive so that we can move on and be free from the weight that unforgiveness carries. My story is filled with dysfunction, but that too is okay because out of that came something beautiful, and God will get the Glory, even out of the dysfunction. Some may feel that your story is too much for people to hear, or for people to be able to identify with, or even understand, but I am here to tell you that there is someone that is waiting to hear YOUR story. YOUR story may be that one that keeps someone off a ledge, a bridge or even pulling the trigger. Let your voice be heard. More importantly, getting it out may just be the healing YOU need.

I struggled for about two years to get this out. I would start and stop. I would take writers' courses and seminar after seminar but could never seem to get it out. God speaks to me a lot through running water, and I would get ideas, and words would be downloaded to me while in the shower, but by the time I get to write them down, what was given would be gone, or not as it was given. I had to really go to

God and ask for help. I know that God gave me this title and this name for a reason, and I know that this story has to be told because there's someone who is waiting to hear my voice, to hear my testimony, and to hear how I made it through. In seeking to become a better me, I was led to a mentor. A mentor that could speak to the innermost recesses of my soul and call out what needed to be awakened and what needed to be put to rest. One that could call me to a higher frequency and speak to my dwindling confidence and rekindle the very little that remained because of what I had gone through. And baby, this version of me, she's unstoppable. She got her confidence back! She is at peace! She is loved! She is ENOUGH! SHE, she is me, and I love her.

So, I want to encourage your hearts just a little more today. No matter what situations you face, you can make it. You are not alone, and God loves you. There is nothing that you can do that will ever stop God from loving you. You were created in His image, and marvelous are God's works. When He went to the cross, He had YOU in mind. Everything that comes to mind, yes, He took that, and that, and yes, that too. He's a faithful and loving God. He will never give us things that we cannot handle. He strengthens us daily. His mercies are new every morning! Great is His faithfulness! Morning by morning, new mercies, I see. All I have needed thine hand has provided. When you don't know what else to do or say, you can just say the name of Jesus. He will never walk out on us, leave us, nor forsake us. While you're going through the storm, keep your eyes and your mind stayed on Jesus, and let Him guide you all the way through.

I pray that something that I have said has touched the hearts of God's people and that the unction of the Holy Spirit has touched you in some way. I encourage you that if you desire to seek Mental Health Services due to the stains of your past, you reach out to someone in your area who may be of some assistance. I come against the stigma of seeking Mental Health services in the Church Community and also in the Black Community as a whole. The devil is a whole liar, and he is defeated. God's people will be free, Mind, Body, and Soul!

Be Blessed, In Jesus' Name!

Made in the USA
Middletown, DE
16 April 2024